FORAGING

THE ESSENTIAL GUIDE TO FREE WILD FOOD

John Lewis-Stempel

RIGHT WAY

Constable & Robinson Ltd
55–56 Russell Square
London WC1B 4HP
www.constablerobinson.com

This edition published by Right Way,
an imprint of Constable & Robinson, 2012

A copy of the British Library Cataloguing in Publication Data
is available from the British Library

ISBN: 978-0-7160-2310-4

Printed and bound in the EU

1   3   5   7   9   10   8   6   4   2

ABOUT THE AUTHOR

John Lewis-Stempel is a forager, farmer and writer. He is the author of the acclaimed *The Wild Life: A Year Spent Living on Wild Food*, described by the *Sunday Telegraph* as 'Fascinating . . . timely and compelling' and by *The Ecologist* as 'A life lesson for us all'.

Other books by John Lewis-Stempel

Fatherhood: The Anthology
England: The Autobiography
The Autobiography of the British Soldier
*Six Weeks: The Short and Gallant Life of the
    British Officer in the First World War*
Young Herriot: The Early Life and Times of James Herriot

CONTENTS

ACKNOWLEDGEMENTS

Thank you to all the following for help and inspiration: Alison Delaney, Andy Hamilton, Judith Mitchell and Duncan Proudfoot at Constable & Robinson, Leslie Peach, Nick Weston. And, naturally, Penny Lewis-Stempel.

DISCLAIMER

Readers are advised that a number of wild plants and mushrooms are poisonous and their ingestion can cause illness, even death. Consequently, it is vitally important that the identity of a mushroom or plant is established beyond doubt before consumption. If the identity of a plant or mushroom is in doubt do not pick or eat it. In some individuals allergic reactions may occur from touching or ingesting non-poisonous plants and mushrooms, and the attention of readers is drawn to the guidelines on trying unfamiliar foods in Chapter 2.

The author and publisher have made every effort to ensure that the information contained in this book is accurate. Information regarding edibility, however, is for guidance only. No legal responsibility can be accepted by the author or publisher for any errors contained in this book, or for any illness, physical or mental reaction or injury arising from information provided, or omitted, herein.

1

WHY EAT WILD FOOD?

Is there such a thing as a free lunch?

Even in the twenty-first century, much of the landscape of Britain is covered by wild plants, many of which are edible. And frequently they are free for the taking.

This book is a guide to the one hundred 'weeds' and mushrooms that are good enough to eat. And, as importantly, you might actually encounter in the great outdoors. There are over 400 'food' plants and mushrooms growing wild in Britain, but some are truly horrible on the tongue, while your chances of bumping into a Silky Volvaria on a walk in the country are slim. More, there are plants, like the Cowslip, now too rare to pick. There is advice in the following pages on recognition – you really don't want to impersonate Lucrezia Borgia and poison all and sundry – but this is, above all, a book about what to do with your foragings, which bits of the plant to use, how to prepare meals and drinks from them, and how to preserve them.

It *is* possible to gather sufficient wild food to make a considerable dent in the household budget; I once lived for a year just on what I could find in the natural larder. This year of living wild in the country required a fulltime Mesolithic lifestyle and few, I suspect, would wish to emulate it (picking sloes from Blackthorn bushes in driving snow for days in a row with fingers scratched to bloody ribbons is definitely not fun) but equally I am sure that a bowl of Nettle Soup, which is in every way delicious, probably tastes just that bit better because you know it cost next to nothing to prepare.

Truth to tell, foraging has many virtues above and beyond penny-saving. In hedges, in parks, and on the coast there are flowers, leaves, nuts, berries and seeds that are 'Superfoods' to rival, even beat, the most exotic fruits of the Amazon jungle. Rosehips contain 20 per cent more vitamin C than an orange, while the humble Hazelnut contains more protein pound for pound than a hen's egg. Many wild plants are highly burgeoningly nutritious. Numerous so-called 'weeds' were once cultivated and have simply fallen out of culinary fashion. Fat Hen and Sorrel are just two such plants to fall by the wayside of changing taste. And the level of nutrition in a wild plant you pick yourself is unlikely to deteriorate much on the walk home, unlike the packaged products of the super-market fruit and veg section, which have the life chilled out of them on a 5,000 mile air journey.

It goes almost without saying that a forager can have a diet unknown to a shopper. When did you last see a Cloudberry or a Pignut in a shop?

Foraging, though, should be as much about mental as physical health. The soul as well as the stomach. Going foraging is a chance to connect with nature, to appreciate and understand it. Simply being outside and seeing green can make a difference to wellbeing; when Henry Thoreau, of *Walden* fame, wrote 'Staying inside the house breeds a sort of insanity always', he was more right than he knew. Modern scientific research shows that the hospital patient exposed to nature, even if it is just the sight of a tree through a window, heals more quickly than the one who is not.

You are never closer to nature than when you are picking it, but the relationship has to be respectful and sustainable. Jumping in a VW camper van and charging around the countryside, snatching a wild food here, there and everywhere as the fancy takes isn't foraging; it's a smash-and-grab raid on nature. Take some time to study your foraging environment, get to know it, and check from time to time on its well-being.

Foraging, of course, is just another way of saying 'hunter-gathering'. Pick a Hazelnut, eat a Blackberry off the bush, roast the roots of Silverweed and you are doing something your prehistoric ancestors did. Literally. They thrived on such foods, and so can you with a little help from this book. There is a definite atavistic pleasure to be had from taking home your first wild food and cooking it. It is a joy way above pulling shrink-wrapped goods off a supermarket shelf. Make a meal of it. To this end, numerous wild food recipes are included in the book, including ones for drinks, from teas to wines. Chapter 13, 'Wild Food By Type', allows you to plan a meal, should you be seeking roots for a starchy filler, leaves for a green vegetable, wild fruit for pudding, herbs for flavouring.

The shortage of Mammoths for the modern spearperson aside, hunting animals is fraught with problems, ethical, legal and technical. But in case you do fancy getting in touch with your inner carnivore, I have suggested some meat-gathering methods open to all: hunting Snails and Shellfish, and picking up road-kill.

Wild food is the ultimate in organic and seasonal. The rhythm of nature is wonderful and reassuring. The botanical clock also means that most wild foods are only available for certain periods of the year. To eat gathered food beyond its season, you will have to preserve it, whether in jams, chutneys, wines, or by drying or freezing. There are instructions too on preserving methods for your gathered bounty.

Foraging as a hobby, as healthy living, or simply as a way of enlivening a walk can be done almost anywhere. It is a misconception that foraging is only for bucolic folk deep in darkest hedgerow country. Wild food is everywhere. On the coast, up mountains, beside rivers, in marshes. My cousin has an allotment in north London; I admire his vegetables, but I could not help but notice that his neighbour's overgrown plot was a running cornucopia of edible weeds. Perhaps the neighbour had discovered the universal truth of gardening: it is so much easier to grow weeds than 'official' vegetables. The boundary of the allotment site (where allotmenteers had discarded unwanted plants in decades gone by) was positively rife with now gone-wild herbs, including Balm, Marjoram, Rosemary, Thyme. Next to the allotment was a suburban garden, with Morel mushrooms growing in the mulch in the herbaceous border. Foraging in the city is likely to be as rewarding as in the countryside; there are 17 plants (plus Snails) listed in Chapter 4 'The Town' and this number of urban edibles could easily have been doubled.

Recognising that people live in different environments, or take their leisure in certain places, I have divided the book by habitat. But no species of plant is so well behaved that it confines itself to, say, just woods. Those Morels growing in a north London garden are proof of that. The divisions are not absolute. This is a guide. You yourself will learn by your practical foraging exactly where the wild things are, the special wasteland corner where Meadowsweet grows, the park ditch loved by Water Mint, the glade in the woods in which Ceps spring up in autumn.

Happy hunter-gathering.

2

WHAT YOU NEED TO KNOW

Foraging, it should go without saying, needs to be safe, legal, and conducted in a way that is sustainable. It should also be fun. And no hobby, surely, could be cheaper. More often than not a carrier bag folded in the pocket and open eyes are all you need. Those, and the ground rules.

Safety

There are a number of poisonous wild plants that can be confused with esculent ones. If you are in doubt over a plant's identity and edibility, leave it out.

A good guide to wild plants and mushrooms is essential, and several are recommended in the Bibliography of this book. Better than relying on a book, take a foraging course or two. There is an online directory of courses at *www.food foragingcourses.co.uk*.

One plant family you do need to be particularly aware of are the Umbellifers, which include such culinary prizes as Hogweed and Cow Parsley – but also the deadly Water Dropwort, Cowbane, Henbane and Hemlock. A good idea is to familiarise yourself absolutely with these four botanical horsemen of the Apocalypse. A better idea still: until you are absolutely confident in your plant identification leave the Umbellifer family alone. Your first mistake with an Umbellifer could well be your last. I have given only scant coverage to edible Umbellifers in this book.

Hemlock, Water Dropwort, Cowbane and Henbane will kill everybody, but some plants only cause illness and reaction in certain individuals. The guilty plants can be surprising; I have come across people who are allergic to Hawthorn berries. It follows that you should initially only try a small amount of a new wild food by placing a small piece on your tongue. Do not ingest. Wait 30 minutes, and see if any allergic reactions occur, such as nausea, hives, or headache.

If all is well, eat a small piece of the plant. Again wait 30 minutes.

There are a few plants that contain chemicals that accumulate negatively in the body, notably those containing oxalic acid. These should not be consumed on a regular basis or in large quantities. So hold back on Sorrel.

Obviously, some care needs to be taken as to where you forage. Unless you are planning a swift exit from the gene pool, scrabbling up or down a seacliff for Rock Samphire is hardly sensible. On the coast take care to know tide times and the location of quicksand; in urban environments, ensure that the foraging site is not harbouring unseen chemicals from extinct heavy industry. Gardens and allotments are both superlative foraging locations – except when sprayed with herbicides and insecticides. Look for tell-tale signs, such as wilting leaves or whitish deposits on the leaves. The verges and hedges of busy roads are certain to be plastered with pollutants from traffic. In the country, do not forage in fields that have been treated to the attentions of agri-chemicals, manure or slurry. Any waterside plants should not be taken if near sewage outlets or industrial polluters. Never forget that the large bush beside a path is likely to be a dog's urinal.

As a rule, wash foraged plants.

Preserving your foraged food depends on having scrupulously sterilised storage vessels and equipment. Bacteria are everywhere, on you, on your wild food, in the air. Even a small infiltration of a harmful bug can spoil a wine, a beer, a jelly or a jam. So before jam-making or brewing, clean all equipment, jars and bottles with warm soapy water using, if necessary, specially shaped nylon bottle-cleaning brushes.

Then sterilise vessels and kit by soaking in diluted 'thin' household beach (25g bleach to 4.5 litres water) or better still in a sterilising solution. Ardent brewers and bottlers use specialist chemical concoction, VWP; easier to obtain are sterilising solutions for baby's bottles, such as Milton Sterilising Fluid.

Do not forget to rinse well before use, since any residue of the sterilising chemical will impart a loathsome aftertaste to your drink or conserve. And imbibing chemicals rather spoils the whole point of gathering, wild, organic food.

The Law
The law on foraging is the proverbial minefield, but the essentials are:

- The digging up of any native plant is illegal, unless 'authorisation' (permission) is first granted by the landowner.

- Under the Wildlife and Countryside Act (1981) it is illegal to uproot, dig up or otherwise interfere with certain endangered species wherever located. The list of these plants (and molluscs) can be consulted at *www.jncc.gov.uk*.

- Special permission is required to forage in national parks and nature reserves, and land owned by the National Trust, Ministry of Defence and the Crown.

- Certain species belong to the Crown. This applies to native Oysters in Scotland.

- A plant is the 'property' of the landowner on which it grows, so permission is necessary to take it or parts of it.

- By the law of trespass, you need permission to enter upon private land.

- Shellfish in some localities belong to commercial enterprises, and if you 'forage' them you are open to the charge of theft.

- Many Shellfish are also subject to closed seasons and rules governing the size they must have attained to be eligible for harvesting, the so-called 'Minimum Landing Size' (MLS). In localities where MLS rules apply, it is an offence (open to prosecution) to take any Shellfish that are smaller than the MLS. The scientific rationale behind MLS is to protect against overfishing, by ensuring that each individual mollusc is allowed to grow to maturity and has a breeding opportunity before being landed.

- Many places have byelaws which ban or control the collecting of wild plants or animals.

- If you go foraging in public with a fixed blade, or a blade longer than 75mm, you are committing a criminal offence with a maximum detention in Her Majesty's prison of four years. Equally, if you have some specialist kit that appears to have been developed for illegal picking you may be considered to be committing a criminal offence. Take a small folding penknife, a modest pair of kitchen scissors and a walking stick instead.

- Despite all the above, foraging plants for your private use is legal under common law. The 'waysides' of roads, paths, canals are generally fair game for foragers, as are parks, commons and tidal waters.

Foraging Etiquette

You should also try to make your foraging ethical by following a few simple codes of foraging conduct:

- Only take what you need, and try to spread your foraging over a wide area, rather than pick from one place. But get to know all your picking places, so you can check the impact of your foraging on the environment. Leave some for other foragers, the birds, bees and animals.

- Do not strip individual plants of their flowers, leaves, fruits or nuts. Gather a few of the edible parts from several plants, using where possible a knife or scissors to remove them. Generally, fungi should be harvested by cutting with a knife at the base.

- Try and disturb the habitat as little as you can.

- Do not remove flowers from annuals and biennials, since the plant needs these to reproduce.

- If possible take positive environmental action by planting the seeds of the foraged plant.

- In addition to the specific plants protected by law under the Wildlife and Countryside Act (1981), the Joint Nature Conservancy Council (JNCC) has issued a longer 'Red List' of threatened species. This can be consulted at *www.jncc.gov.uk*.

Equipment

A carrier bag will do for many foraging expeditions, but a 'trug' or wide basket is preferable for leaves and most berries, since the air can circulate and the goodies don't get squished. That said, you may still need to tie a carrier bag over the top to stop leaves blowing away. I'm not convinced that anything better has yet been made for Blackberry picking than a washed-out plastic ice cream container.

Generally, mushrooms, leaves, flowers and seed heads need to be cut off, so a folding gardening knife or smallish kitchen scissors is a must buy. There are specialist mushroom knives to purchase if you get seriously into mushrooming. A stiff paint brush to whisk off dirt is a good idea.

The Number 1 rule of foraging is that the nicest fruit is always furthest away, and highest up. Take a walking stick. If PC Plod accuses you of going prepared for felonious scrumping, develop a quick limp.

The Number 2 rule of foraging is that some choice fruits are surrounded by thorns designed by the lovechild of Lucifer and the Marquis de Sade. Sea Buckthorn, Rosehips and Sloes (from the Blackthorn), among others, will require leather gardening gloves for picking. Nettles, naturally, require rubber gloves to save your hands from stinging. The longer they go up the arm the better.

To recap, a foraging kit list includes:

A guide to wild plants and mushrooms
Carrier bags
Walking stick
Trug/recycled ice-cream container
Folding gardening knife/Mushroom knife
Brush
Pair of kitchen scissors
Leather gloves/Rubber gloves

If you are heading for the coast, take a child's bucket and spade, plus a rake, to harvest Shellfish.

The Seasons

Foraging is a natural activity, regulated by the sun and the rotation of the earth. There is not a thing you can do to change the seasonal round. Some plants flourish in certain times only, a handful can be found throughout the year. Oddly, when you get used to seasonality – the fact that, unlike on the supermarket shelf, certain produce in nature is not available at your beck and call – looking for the first occurrence of a plant becomes part of the fun. There's a lot to be said for the circadian clock.

No season in Britain fails to provide food, though you may be surprised by just how little wild food is to be foraged at the end of a dry summer. Wait a week or two, however, and you have the hedgerow harvest of autumn when your biggest headache is likely to be what to do with all the Blackberries.

Seasonality is also rather relative. The north of Scotland is at least two botanical weeks behind Torquay. Equally, the hill on which I live in the Welsh Borders is two weeks behind in the flowering of Blackthorn than the bottom of the valley.

To give the reader a rough idea of what to find when, there is a Forager's Calendar in Chapter 12.

3

CHILDREN AND FORAGING

If you care to think about it, foraging is a species of treasure-hunting. Is there a child who does not want to go seeking treasure?

Spotting natural edible 'treasures' can be a fool-proof way of enlivening one of those constitutionals that adults consider necessary for children. Equally, foraging is an engaging activity for children in its own right, particularly if they make their gathered wild goods into breakfast, lunch or dinner. Take time too to explain to them the natural ways of the plant or mollusc you are gathering, its role in the environment, and what animals eat it besides yourself. A wealth of children's literary classics are set in the British countryside; foraging allows an enhanced appreciation of those books, as well as equipping a child with some serious chips in the game of playground one-upmanship, such as the derivation of the name for the gnome Baldmoney in *The Little Grey Men* by 'BB'. Much more than this, the outdoors is a place rich in food for the imagination of children.

It goes without saying that a child out foraging is beating 'Nature Deficit Disorder', to borrow the term coined by American writer Richard Louv to describe the increasing dislocation between children and nature. A child introduced to the wonders of nature is a child likely to become an adult with a passion for the environment.

When foraging with children, double check you are

following all the rules on safety outlined in Chapter 2. Moreover: Do not let them forage alone, and do not let them see you foraging any plants which have dangerous lookalikes. In particular, do not forage Umbellifers with children. With children forage the unmistakably easy, such as Dandelions and Blackberries. Indeed, if you are an absolute foraging beginner yourself, go for obvious plants, because trying to distinguish certain esculent plants can be frustratingly tricky and you don't want to become dispirited. The more you forage, the more you will learn which plant is which. In the meantime, harvest plants that are easy to identify, easy to find, easy to cook. Try starting with Nettles.

Make sure too, that a child is adequately dressed and booted. A cold child is not a happy child, and a child stung by Nettles is positively miserable.

Lastly, one does not need to be a professor of sociology to see that a family (however construed) that forages together stays together. There is nothing more basic than the finding of food. Foraging binds a family together in purpose and familiarity. And, yes, in fun.

4

THE TOWN

BORAGE   *Borago officinalis*
Local Names: BEE-BREAD, BURRAGE, TALEWORT, COOL-TANKARD, BLUE STARS
Season: May–September

Like numerous other herbs introduced to Britain by the Romans, Borage has long since escaped the kitchen garden. Today it is found running feral in wasteland, the edges of allotments, abandoned gardens and anywhere where once proud owners have dumped it, sometimes existing in large colonies and usually favouring a sunny aspect. The plant can grow to 75cm in height, and the stems and the dull oval leaves are lightly hairy.

'Borage' is derived from the Latin *borra*, meaning 'rough hair'. Intensely blue star-shaped flowers appear between June and September. The Old Masters often chose Borage blue for the Madonna's cloak. The flowers, as with those of **Balm**, are addictively attractive to bees. One of Borage's country names is 'Bee-bread'.

The sweet flowers make good human food too. They can be added to a salad, candied like those of **Sweet Violet**, used as decoration, as nibble, fried as fritters. No English summer is complete without Borage flowers floating in a glass of Pimms No. 1, white wine or lemonade. Young leaves – which have a mild cucumber flavour – can also be immersed in drinks.

They are good too in salads. Otherwise, add to soft cheese (after shredding) for a sandwich spread, or fry in olive oil – when you remove from the pan judiciously dash the Borage leaves with lemon juice. In Basque and Ligurian cookery, Borage leaves have a starring role in casseroles and frittatas, usually accompanied by a chorus of peppery, spicy sausage.

Borage is part of the *Boraginaceae* family and is related to **Comfrey**. During ancient and medieval times Borage was grown extensively as a medicinal plant, in the belief that it induced bravery and happiness. According to Dioscorides, Borage was the essential ingredient in *nepenthe*, the Homeric herb wine which famously induced pleasant forgetfulness. Crusaders were given Borage for courage in stirrup-cups before departing to the Holy Land. The belief in Borage's ability to bring on bliss lingered on into the Elizabethan age. Nicholas Culpeper in his *Herbal* declared that Borage 'purgeth melancholie'.

BORAGE STEW

Serves 4

In the Basque country, Borage is known as the 'Queen of Vegetables', and is combined in stews with chorizo and red kidney beans.

500g Borage leaves
3 tbsp extra virgin olive oil
200g chorizo, sliced
1 medium onion, diced
2 cloves garlic, sliced
1 tsp cayenne pepper
750ml stock
salt
300g red kidney beans, cooked

Clean and coarsely chop the Borage leaves, and boil in an inch of water for 5 minutes. Heat the olive oil in a saucepan, add the sliced sausage, onion, garlic and cayenne, and fry for a minute or two. Then add the stock, a large pinch of salt and the kidney beans and bring to the boil.

Take the Borage off the heat, drain, squeeze, and chop finely. Place in the saucepan with the other ingredients and simmer for 10 minutes. Serve with crusty bread.

BURDOCK *Arctium minus*

Local Names: WILD RHUBARB, SWEETHEARTS, BACHELORS' BUTTONS, CUCKOO BUTTONS, COCKLE DOCK, GIPSY'S RHUBARB, TUZZY MUZZY, TURKEY RHUBARB
Season: May–June (leaves and stems)
Throughout the year (roots)

That ubiquitous Stuart herbalist Nicholas Culpeper considered Burdock 'so well known even to the little Boys, who pull off the Burs to throw and stick upon one another, that I spare to write any description of it.'

If the purple prickly heads of Burdock are not well-known to you the biennial has another useful identifier: its large leaves, with their heart-shaped base, are very like those of rhubarb.

Found on wasteland, scrub, roadsides (particularly if damp), stream and woodland edges, Burdock is a plant of many useful parts. Young leaves can be cooked like spinach, the stems can be steamed like asparagus, or deep fried, while the long tap root makes a fine vegetable; in Japan, where Burdock is grown commercially, the root is chopped into matchsticks and boiled. Alternatively, the 'matchsticks' can be soaked in water then stir fried, or parboiled and sautéed in butter. The taste of both root and stems is of a bitter celery.

And, yes, the root can also be used to make **Dandelion** and Burdock beer. This drink was reputedly invented by the theologian St Thomas Aquinas in the thirteenth century; on walking from his place of prayer, Aquinas trusted to God to provide his needs. After concocting a drink from the first plants he encountered, so stimulating did Aquinas find his patented Dandelion and Burdock beer that it helped him formulate the thoughts that became the bases of his master-piece, *Summa Theologica*.

Aquinas' drink was mildly alcoholic, a type of mead. Somewhere in the course of history, the British did the inverse of alchemy and turned it into a soft drink.

One note of warning. Aquinas may have found Dandelion and Burdock a stimulant of the brain, but a legion of medieval herbalists considered it a provoker of lust.

DANDELION AND BURDOCK BEER

The alcoholic content of this beer varies, but may reach 8%, even more.

110g fresh Burdock root, finely chopped
450g Nettle leaves
110g Dandelion leaves, chopped
4.5 litres water
550g white sugar
2 tbsp dry cider
ale yeast

Equipment (sterilised before use)
large saucepan/cauldron
large wooden spoon
muslin
fermentation bin
bottles
siphoning tube

Place the Burdock, Nettles and Dandelion in a cauldron and add 2.25 litres of water. Bring to the boil and simmer for 30 minutes. Add the sugar and stir to dissolve. Take off the heat and strain through the muslin to remove the solids. Pour into the fermentation bin and add the remaining water, the cider and yeast. Leave to ferment in a warm place for ten days. Siphon into bottles. Let it condition for a week. Drink within three weeks.

DANDELION AND BURDOCK CORDIAL

And for the children, an alcohol-free Dandelion and Burdock drink.

2 tsp ground Dandelion root
2 tsp ground Burdock root
1.5 litres water
2cm root ginger, sliced
1 whole star anise
1 lemon
600g caster sugar

Equipment
large saucepan/cauldron
coffee grinder/mortar and pestle
muslin
funnel
bottles (sterilised before use)

Dry the Dandelion and Burdock roots by cutting into 5cm segments and sticking in the oven on a low heat for 1–2 hours with oven door slightly ajar, turning every half hour.

Take out and grind to a fine powder in a coffee mill or a keep-fit pestle-and-mortar.

Meanwhile, bring the water to the boil. Add in the powdered Dandelion, Burdock, ginger, star anise and juice of the lemon. Simmer for 20 minutes, then add the sugar and stir until dissolved. Allow to cool, then strain into bottles through the muslin, which should be folded over several times inside the funnel.

Serve one part cordial to four parts water. If you want fizz, use soda water instead of mineral water.

WARM BURDOCK AND PIGEON SALAD

Serves 4

45g Burdock root
4 large handfuls of mixed spring salad, such as
  Chickweed, Hairy Bittercress, Corn Salad,
  Nipplewort, Hawthorn
olive oil
8 pigeon breasts

For the dressing:
4 tsp Beech or olive oil
1 tsp salt
4 tsp red wine
4 tsp pan juice

Clean the Burdock root and slice into long matchsticks. Simmer in lightly salted water for 15 minutes, allowing the water to evaporate.

Wash the salad leaves.

When the Burdock is nearly dry, heat the oil to smoking point and fry the pigeon breasts for 2 minutes each side, which will leave them nicely bloody inside. (If you want to follow Health and Safety advice, or are not absolutely sure of your pigeons' provenance, cook until the juices run clear, about 3 minutes each side.)

Take the Burdock and pigeons off the heat and leave both to cool for 5 minutes.

Mix the salad dressing, not forgetting to add the teaspoons of pan juice. Slice the pigeon breasts into three lengthways.

Put the Burdock matches on the plates, arrange the salad on top. Carefully lay the sliced pigeon breasts over this green bed. Dribble the dressing over.

CARAWAY *Carum Carvi*
Season: June–August

Caraway is a herb with heritage. The chefs of Richard II included Caraway in the medieval cookbook *A Forme of Cury*, and in Shakespeare's *Henry IV* Falstaff is offered a 'pippin and dish of caraways'. Caraway – in the shape of 'comfits', being Carraway seeds coated in sugar – was the standard Elizabethan way of finishing off a feast. Caraway was believed to prevent indigestion and flatulence – as well as tantalize the tongue. Not until Edwardian times did the British fall out of love with it.

Caraway plants growing wild in Britain are descendants of those that once graced herb gardens, so look for it amidst ruins, wasteland and neglected allotments. A member of the Umbellifer family, Caraway is tall with feathery leaves. It likes sun and free-draining soil.

All parts of the plant are edible. Young spring leaves impart an aniseed flavour to salads and soups, and the autumn root of a second year plant can be boiled, baked or roasted, just as you would do with carrots. Most sought after, however, are the aromatic brown 'seeds' (technically, fruits) that appear in mid-summer. Harvest the seeds about a month after the white flowers have faded and the seeds are turning brown. Cut the stems after rain or dew (so ripe seeds don't scatter), and place upside down in a paper bag in an airy place for about 3–4 weeks, by which time the seeds will have dried and fallen to the bottom of the bag. Store them in air-tight containers. Former spice jars are ideal.

When harvesting, remember to leave some seed heads on the plant.

The culinary uses of the seed are myriad and fabulous. Sprinkle over pork and lamb, and put in with potatoes and cabbage. (The Germans regularly put Caraway in sauerkraut.) In baking, Caraway seeds can be added to biscuits and buns, bread and apple pie.

GINGERBREAD NUTS

The recipe is the venerable Mrs Beaton's, from her famous book of *Household Management*.

55g butter
450g treacle
125g coarse brown sugar
55g ground ginger
25g candied orange angelica   } **cut into very small**
25g candied orange peel   } **pieces but not**
15g candied lemon peel   } **bruised**
15g Caraway seeds, pounded
15g Coriander seeds, pounded
1 egg
flour

Melt the butter in a small pan. Put the treacle into a basin, and pour over it the melted butter, the sugar and ginger. Stir these ingredients well together, and whilst mixing, add the candied angelica and peel, and the Caraway and Coriander seeds.

Having mixed it all thoroughly together, break in an egg, and work the whole mixture together with as much flour as is necessary to form a paste. Roll this out and stamp into nuts of any size and put them on a tin plate, and bake in a slow oven (150°C/Gas Mark 2) from 15–30 minutes.

CHICKWEED   *Stellaria media*

Local Names: WHITE BIRD'S EYE, CHICKENWEED, WINTER-WEED, STAR WEED, CHICKEN'S MEAT
Season: Throughout the year, but best February–May

Young poultry and caged birds, as you might guess, are said to thrive on this common annual. So too pigs, who grow speedily on its high protein (15–20 per cent) and iron content. But Chickweed is not just for the birds and the pigs. It is fit for humans too, making a useful salad, or a chopped and colourful addition to pasta and risotto dishes, or a steamed green vegetable, or a soup. The taste is reminiscent of spinach. Chickweed pesto and Chickweed pakoras have much to recommend them.

Although a tough little plant, Chickweed does not enjoy frosts; otherwise, you are likely to find mats of creeping Chickweed the year round in gardens and on wasteland, making it one of the forager's most loyal friends. Cut the leaves and stems with scissors; otherwise you are left with much root washing. The flower is a distinctive five-petal white star ('stellaria'), which acts as a natural barometer, opening when the weather will be good, closing up when it will be bad. A sure clue to Chickweed's identification is a single line of fine hairs running up the stem.

Chickweed has long been an item in the medicinal cupboard, as well as in the pantry. Nicholas Culpeper proposed Chickweed as an anti-inflammatory, and the plant's juices are reputed to be efficacious in the treatment of skin and eye complaints. The plant is employed in many herbal weight-loss formulas because it contains high amounts of saponins, which are claimed to be dissolvers of fat cells and reducers of cholesterol.

CHICKWEED AND FETA SALAD

Serves 4

2 cloves garlic, minced
2 tbsp lemon juice
2 tbsp extra virgin olive oil
pepper
¼ tsp freshly grated ginger
400g Chickweed
400g Feta, crumbled
200g Kalamari olives

Mix the dressing of garlic, lemon juice, olive oil, pepper and ginger.

Toss the Chickweed, Feta and Kalamari olives together. Pour over the dressing. Serve.

CLEAVERS   *Galium aparine*

Local Names: GOOSEGRASS, CLIVERS, STICKY BILLY, KISS-
ME-QUICK, GOSLING SCROTH, BEDSTRAW, CATCHWEED,
STICKY BUD
Season: February–May

When you were a child, Cleavers were the long green tendrils
you silently attached to the coat backs of friends, hoping they
would not notice.

Cleavers is an annual herb whose ability to scramble up
vegetation – and stick to coats – comes virtue of thousands of
tiny hooks. It likes a sunny, open aspect. Invariably, Cleavers
appears not singly but in huge battalions, and will form dense
mats up hedges and over neglected ground. It chokes the life
out of any plant life it encounters. Cleavers appears early in
the year, and can be cut – or pulled up if you are a gardener –
and then stripped of its leaves. Steam or boil briefly in slightly
salted water for a green vegetable.

The roots produce a red dye, and the roasted fruit can be
substituted for coffee – appropriately enough, as Cleavers is
related to the coffee plant. However, you will need armfuls of
the late season plant to thrash onto a hard surface to release
enough of the fruits (small burrs) to make worthwhile coffee.
Try instead: a herbal infusion made from soaking handfuls of
the leaves overnight in cold water. This tonic has many
virtues, it is said, from removing excess toxins after excessive
imbibing to removing excess fat from the midriff. Back in the
sixteenth century, Cleavers was used in slimming regimes,
much as **Chickweed** is today. According to the herbalist John
Gerard, 'women do usually make pottage of Cleavers with a
little mutton and oatmeal, to cause lankenesse, and to keep
them from fatness'.

On the other hand, armfuls of the plant were fed to goslings
to fatten them up.

COLTSFOOT *Tussilago farfara*
Local Names: COUGHWORT, HALLFOOT, HORSEHOOF, ASS'S FOOT, FOALSWORTH, FIELDHOVE, BULLSFOOT
Season: February–April

A member of the Daisy family, Coltsfoot is one of the first plants to flower in the year, popping up at the same times as crocuses. The flowers, which are a sweetly delicious raw ingredient in salad or as a base for wine, are a bright, startling yellow and appear long before the large hoof-shaped leaves. The latter can be put into a salad in June and July.

Coltsfoot, for all its beauty, tends to like rough places to hang out. Seek it in waste ground, building sites, roadsides, the edge of woods, remembering that it has a preference for heavy clay.

A hardy perennial, Coltsfoot reaches 30cm in height. The herb's botanical name comes from 'tussis', meaning 'cough-dispeller'. The Greeks and Romans smoked the dried leaves, and Coltsfoot is still an ingredient in herbal tobacco. Coltsfoot Rock Stick (a hardboiled sweet containing extracts of the herb) and Coltsfoot tea have both long been cottage cures for coughs. An alcoholic wine and a beer made from Coltsfoot also have an expectoral purpose.

DANDELION *Taraxacum officinale*
Local Names: CLOCK, CLOCK FLOWER, GOLDEN SUNS, FAIRY COCKS, DEVIL'S MILK PLANT, PISS-A-BED, WET-A-BED
Season: April–June (leaves and flowers)
October–February (roots)

Who does not know Dandelion, possessor of the single sunny head, toothed leaves and spherical 'clocks' of seeds? The Dandelion is one of the commonest perennial 'weeds', and offers good foraging because root, leaves and flowers can be put to plentiful culinary uses.

Dandelion is abundant throughout the northern hemisphere in lawns, gardens, wasteland, road verges and meadows.

The plant's long serrated leaves are responsible for its name, being a corruption of the French 'dents-de-lion' or lion's teeth, which they are fancied to resemble. In spring and summer pick leaves from the centre of the rosette of young plants and use as salad after washing thoroughly. The Stuart diarist John Evelyn adored Dandelion leaf salad, believing: 'With this homely salley Hecate entertained Theseus.' For a quick spring salad that Evelyn would have enjoyed, tear and mix young Dandelion leaves, **Hazel** shoots, **Garlic Mustard**, then toss with oily vinaigrette. Serve on top of thinly sliced tomatoes.

In Italy, blanched Dandelion leaves, with anchovies, garlic, capers, olives, and pine kernels, make a peasant's pie known as *pizza di scarola*.

All Dandelion leaves have a tendency to bitterness; young leaves are the least acrid. All Dandelion leaves can be made mellower still by blanching them in cold water for an hour or three. Old leaves can be steamed like spinach.

The golden flower of the Dandelion is often overlooked by foragers, but try one raw, deep fried as a fritter, or use to brew beer or make a light white wine in springtime when the flowers are at their most abundant. Even more neglected are the buds, which can be pickled as a substitute for the buds of the caper bush. For a sensation on the other, far side of the taste spectrum pick the unopened buds, dunk in sugar syrup, and heat to reduce.

To dig up the long tapering roots of the Dandelion you will need a spade because they can be a challenging foot or more long. The roots are at their fattest in autumn and winter, when they make an excellent vegetable. To remove bitterness cut up into 4–5cm sections and boil for 15 minutes, change the water and boil for another five.

Dandelion has distinct diuretic qualities, as recognised by local names 'Piss-a-bed' and 'Wet-a-bed'. In France it is known as *pissenlit*, in Italy as *pissialetto*.

Chicory (*Cichorium intybus*) is the close edible cousin of Dandelion, and can be used in the same ways, nutty bitter leaves for salad, roots for coffee and vegetable. In many countries chicory coffee is a popular drink; in Britain chicory has long been blended with 'real' coffee. 'Chicory' is an Anglicization of the Arabic *chicouryeh*. The Romans knew it as *cichorium*. Some British localities know it as 'Coffee Weed'.

Chicory will grow anywhere relatively dry and open, and is often to be found near derelict cottages. In summer the perennial is easily identified by its blue daisy-type flowers, but by then its leaves are mouth-pucker bitter. Among the Romans, Chicory enjoyed the reputation as a panacea. Among botanists, it enjoys the reputation of being a 'flower clock'. Linnaeus found that the blooms of Chicory planted in his native Uppsala, Sweden, opened at midsummer at 5am and closed at 10pm on the dot.

DANDELION COFFEE

Dandelion roots, like those of Chicory, make a coffee substitute, one which has the distinct advantage of not containing caffeine. The taste is nutty and bitter. Calculate that 4.5 litres of raw roots will produce 1 litre of coffee. Do not bother to peel roots, simply wash in water and if any attached soil is particularly recalcitrant use a washing-up brush. Pat roots dry, then cut into 5cm lengths. Place on a baking tray in the centre of the oven and roast at 190°C/Gas Mark 5 for about 1–2 hours, turning every half hour to ensure even roasting. Leave the oven door slightly ajar to let out moisture. Watch like the proverbial hawk, and be prepared to whip some bits out before others. Allow to cool, then pulverise in a grinder. Generally, Dandelion coffee matches ground Arabica coffee in strength, so a level teaspoon per cup.

Use exactly the same recipe for Chicory coffee.

DANDELION WINE

A classic wine of the British countryside, to be made on St George's Day, 23 April, when the flowers of the Dandelion star the lawn, the verge and the meadow.

1.5 litres Dandelion flowers
2 lemons
1 orange
4.5 litres water
2kg sugar
champagne yeast
1 tsp yeast nutrient

Equipment (sterilised before use)
large saucepan, or witches' cauldron
fermentation bin
4.5 litre demi-john
airlock and bung
funnel
spoon
muslin

Snip the green stems off the back of the flowers since these will bitter the wine. Scrape the skin off the lemons and orange with a potato peeler, ensuring no white pith comes with the shavings.

Put the heads into the fermentation bin, cover with 4.5 litres of boiling water and cover loosely with muslin cloth.

Leave for three days, then strain into a large saucepan, add the sugar, and peeling from the fruits. Bring to the boil, then simmer gently for 10 minutes.

Pour into a sterile fermentation bin, add the juice of the orange and lemons. When the liquid has cooled to baby washing point (when you can dip in your elbow comfortably), sprinkle in the yeast and yeast nutrient.

Cover with muslin and leave until fermentation slows, about 8–10 days. Siphon into a demijohn and allow to ferment out. Rack. Bottle when fermentation has ceased. Allow to mature for a year in the bottle.

DANDELION SALAD

Serves 4

4 strips bacon
1 tbsp extra virgin olive oil
20–30 young Dandelion leaves, washed
2 hardboiled eggs, sliced
salt and pepper
cider vinegar

Fry the bacon strips in the oil until crisp, then crunch to bits and place to one side. In the hot pan, lay the Dandelion leaves and stir over medium heat until they have wilted, which will take a minute or so. They will splatter during frying, so take care. Put equal amounts onto four plates, top with the crumbled bacon and sliced egg. Sprinkle with salt, pepper and vinegar and serve immediately.

DOCK   *Rumex obtusifolius/Rumex crispus*

Local Names: KETTLE DOCK, BUTTER DOCK
Season: March–May

Nettle out, dock in
Dock remove the nettle sting.

The use of the Broad-leaved Dock (*Rumex obtusifolius*) in soothing Nettle stings on children's skin is old and venerable; Chaucer refers to it in *Troilus and Crisede*, written c. 1380. The Dock has culinary uses too: pick very young leaves and substitute for cabbage, either boiling twice or cooking in slightly sugared water to lessen the bitterness. Or try frying in butter with Dandelion leaves. The country name of Butter Dock refers to the plant's use as a wrapping for . . . butter. The British dish of 'dock pudding' is confusingly made from the leaves of **Bistort**, not Docks.

This commonest of weeds, to be found everywhere, even in central London, has a high oxalic acid content – which impairs absorption of minerals – so sufferers of gout, rheumatism and renal disease should imbibe with moderation.

The less common Curled Dock (*Rumex crispus*) is found in many of the same wasteland, hedge and garden abodes as the Broad-leaved Dock, though it does like to be beside the seaside. The appropriately wavy margins to its leaves help distinguish it from its Broad-leaved cousin. Many foragers, myself included, prefer Curled to Broad on the plate.

STUFFED DOCK LEAVES
An English version of stuffed vine leaves.

Gather 10–20 young Dock leaves, wash, and pat dry with a tea towel.

Make a stuffing consisting of cooked rice, grated cheese, chopped cooked **Comfrey** and seasoning, and mix well. Put a large teaspoonful of the stuffing on the Dock leaf and roll it up. Secure with a toothpick, brush with olive oil, put in an ovenproof dish and bake at 180°C/Gas Mark 4 for 25 minutes.

GROUND ELDER *Aegopodium podagraria*
Local Names: GOUTWEED, HERB GERRARD, ASHWEED, GROUND ASH, GOAT'S FOOT, FARMER'S PLAGUE, BISHOP'S WEED.
Season: April–June

Ground Elder is a weed dismally familiar to gardeners. As long ago as the sixteenth century John Gerard was complaining, 'Once taken roote it will hardly be gotten out again, spoiling and getting every yeere more ground.' Give Ground Elder an inch and it will take a yard, especially if that yard is damp and shady. Look for it also on wasteland, under hedges and at the edge of woods.

The gardener's revenge on Ground Elder is to serve it up in

a dish. A perennial pot-herb imported by the Romans, Ground Elder has leaves and shoots with a pungent strong parsley-ish taste. Pick in spring and early summer before the plant flowers, and boil or steam as a green vegetable. Leaves can also be chopped and added to omelettes and fritters.

The plant, found throughout the realm, grows up to 1m tall. Leaves are divided into three lobes which together look a little like a hoof mark; 'Aegepodium' is Greek for 'goat's foot'. Ground Elder has white flowers, arranged in umbels on a hollow stem.

In days of yore, Ground Elder was held to be good for relieving the symptoms of gout. Since ecclesiasts were believed to be chronic sufferers of the disease (on account of their taste for wine and rich food), the folk name of Bishop's Weed followed as a matter of course.

GROUND ELDER SOUP

Serves 4

2 large handfuls of Ground Elder leaves
100g butter
50g flour
550ml vegetable stock
300ml cream
salt and pepper

Wash the leaves, and cook in the melted butter for 10–15 minutes, stirring frequently. Add the flour, and stir in the stock gradually until the mixture thickens. Put in a blender and blast. Return to the saucepan, add the cream and seasoning. Heat gently. Serve hot.

HAIRY BITTERCRESS   *Cardamine hirsuta*
Local Names: POPPING CRESS, HAIRY CRESS
Season: February–November

Hairy Bittercress is a weed in need of renaming since it is
neither obviously hairy, nor remotely bitter. Look instead for
a low, rosette-shaped plant whose leaves have a pleasant
peppery flavour reminiscent of rocket, making it indispensable in a wild green salad.

Hairy Bittercress is one of the first plants to burst forth in
spring, and is particularly fond of cultivated ground.
Gardeners loathe it. In a bad year for them, but a good year for
the forager, the drab rounded leaves and white diamante
flowers (usually seen from March to August) of Hairy
Bittercress will carpet the earth so that it will become
occluded. Because of its explosive seed pods (which shoot
their 20 contents one metre or more), Hairy Bittercress
spreads with imperial ambition. So, do a gardener a favour
and pull up Hairy Bittercress by the roots. To eat, simply snip
off the roots and wash the rosette. Aside from adding to salad,
put it in a cheese or egg sandwich. Or place it by itself
between bread slices with a dribble of French dressing.

In its way, the persistence of Hairy Bittercress is admirable.
It can be found at over 1000m and in the depths of winter,
although the taste and texture of the leaflets coarsen as the
year rolls past. As well as gardens, it can be found living
happily in greenhouses, beside railway lines, and on waste
ground.

Hairy Bittercress is a close relative of the equally esculent
Wavy Bittercress (*Cardamine flexuosa*), whose flowers have
six stamens, whereas Hairy Bittercress's have four. Wavy
Bittercress is also, at 23cm, slightly larger. Wintercress,
meanwhile, shares only the colloquial English word for a
small green salad plant, 'cress', with Hairy Bittercress;
Wintercress is actually a species of rocket. In many countries
Wintercress is named for St Barbara (hence its scientific name
of *Barbarea vulgaris*), probably because her festival is 4
December when this remarkable, glossy green herb is still

going strong in the garden and on wasteland, making it one of the few greens to be foraged in the days of northern darkness. Wintercress is rich in vitamin C and A, and was used as an anti-scorbutic before citrus fruits were imported by the ship-load. The large-lobed leaves, arranged in a rosette, are best before the yellow flowers appear (in some localities it is known as 'Yellow Rocket') and can be added to salads with alacrity.

LAMB'S LETTUCE   *Valerianella locusta*
Local Names: RABBIT'S LETTUCE, CORN SALAD, FIELD SALAD
Season: January–October

This member of the Valerian family appears as early as January, around the same time as the first lambs pop out, a chronological coincidence captured in the plant's name. The oblong leaves are gathered together in a tight cluster, and the plant will grow up to 10cm in height.

Lamb's Lettuce used to be a staple foodstuff of English medieval peasants, who cultivated it in plots. John Evelyn, the English diarist, recommended the use of 'corn-sallet' in 1699 and historically the plant's main use has been as green salad or flavouring in soups.

Keep it simple in the kitchen. The somewhat nutty leaves are perfect in salads, with a touch of French dressing. Or steam like spinach and serve with a knob of butter and a pinch of pepper.

Lamb's Lettuce is the mortal enemy of gardeners, due to its habit of infesting the rows between vegetables. It is not fussy about its habit; as well as the vegetable plot, it will happily colonize the roadside verge, railway bank and arable field. We have it growing in the cracks between the stones of our house.

In some versions of the German fairy tale 'Rapunzel' it is Lamb's Lettuce, rather than Rampion Bellflower (*Campanula rapunculus*), that is grown by the wicked witch and craved by the childless woman.

LIME *Tilia cordata/Tilia europaea*
Local Names: LIND, LINDEN
Season: June–July

Lime is a tall, dome-shaped deciduous tree native to the northern hemisphere. The yellowish flowers, which appear in mid-summer, are heavily scented and are one of the main reasons for the widespread ornamental planting of the tree alongside city streets and in parks. Some manor houses had Lime walks and pergolas, where the branches were woven overhead to provide an all round olfactory sensation.

Lime or Linden tea, made from the dried flowers, captures the honey-like essence of the flowers, and makes for a calming drink. Use about one dessertspoonful of dried leaves to 0.5 litres of boiling water, and leave to infuse for several minutes. Do not add milk to the pale, delicately scented liquor, although those with a sweet tooth might appreciate a spoonful of honey.

Lime flowers can also be used to flavour liqueurs, Pimms No 1, homemade lemonade, cordial, as well as to make a light wine.

Like the Birch tree, Lime produces satisfying amounts of sap when 'tapped'. To tap a Lime tree in spring, when the sap begins to rise (as signalled by the appearance of small wrapped parcels of leaves on the tree) first find a Lime tree with a diameter of at least 25cm; any less than that, and the tree might be too puny to spare its lifeblood. Drill a hole in the trunk at a 30 degree angle, just penetrating below the bark and no bigger than the plastic tubing you need to stick in the tree to siphon off the sap; the other end of the tubing goes into a demi-john or large mineral water bottle at ground level. After a day or two, sap should be collecting in the receptacle.

Tapping trees in an urban area can be tricky. Aside from the small matter of permission, anything visible on public property is likely to be interfered with. The forager Fergus Drennan suggests drilling the hole well above head height, and draining the sap into a plastic bottle tied to the trunk or a convenient branch.

Wherever you tap a tree you must plug the hole on finishing. A thick twig hammered in will do. Plugging reduces the possibility of infection entering the Lime through what is, after all, an open wound.

The Lime tree is rich in lore. In the age of chivalry, the Lind was the tree of love; in the twentieth century, its wood provided the frames for Mosquito aircraft of World War II. Most appositely, the botanist Carl Linnaeus owed his surname to the Linden tree outside the family home.

LIME SAP WINE
4.5 litres Lime sap
250ml white grape concentrate
1kg sugar
2 tsp citric acid
½ tsp tannin
1 packet hock wine yeast

Equipment (sterilised before use)
large saucepan, or better still the sort of cauldron a
**   witch would use**
fermentation bin
piece of muslin
2 x 4.5 litre demijohns
siphoning tube
airlock and bung

Put the sap, concentrate and sugar into the saucepan and bring to the boil. Remove from the heat, add the citric acid, then stir vigorously to dissolve the sugar. Allow to cool to room temperature, then stir in the tannin, pour into the fermentation bin and sprinkle the yeast on top. Cover loosely with a piece of muslin and leave for ten days or so.

Siphon into a demijohn and rack after a month. Allow the fermentation to finish before bottling. Age for three months minimum.

ORACHE *Atriplex patula*
Local Names: IRON ROOT, MUCKWEED, DUNGWEED
Season: April–September

Some say 'Oar-atch', some say 'Or-ash', some say 'O-raitch'. There is also disagreement over whether there should be an 'e' as a nomenclatural appendage; you will see the same plant spelt 'Orach'. Probably the odd name of this annual plant is a French corruption of 'Atriplex', in turn corrupted in Anglo-Saxon into Orach/e.

However pronounced or written, *Atriplex patula* is a weed widespread in wasteland, on roadsides and on the coast of southern England, and close-enough in the look of its triangular leaves to **Fat Hen** to share the folk names of 'Dungweed' and 'Muckweed'. The young leaves can be used as pot-herb (its historical usage), or like spinach, or as salad.

Do not use the roots, which are mildly toxic. There is also a similar inedible species – *Atriplex littoralis*. This, however, has a foul smell, and fouler taste.

RIBWORT PLANTAIN
Plantago lanceolata
Local Names: CANARY SEED, SNAKEWEED, RATSTAIL, CUCKOO'S BREAD, HEALING BLADE
Season: April–June

If a plant has a multitude of folk names it is a sure sign that humans have found it useful over the centuries. Ribwort Plantain is no exception to the rule, being long venerated as a styptic and antibiotic for scratches (apply Plantain leaves, crushed), an anti-inflammatory for insect bites (ditto), and a green fodder for poultry. Humans can eat Plantain too, although the plant's bitterness and fibrosity make it a hard-to-acquire taste. Use only young leaves, and steam to within an inch of their life. If one can stomach this perennial, its virtue is that it is packed with vitamins C and K, plus flavonoids and polysaccharides.

Found in lawns, wasteland, roadsides and parks, Ribwort Plaintain is one of our commonest plants, and is easily identified by its rosette of basal leaves, the latter having long parallel veins or 'ribs'. The minute flowers are arranged in a vertical spike that reaches up to 45cm in height and does indeed look unpleasantly like a rat's tail.

There are two similar species, Greater Plantain (*P. Major*) and Sea Plantain (*P. Maritime*), both of which are also edible. If you are in a survival situation.

SHAGGY INK CAP   *Coprinus comatus*
Local Name: LAWYER'S WIG
Season: September–November

Probably the most useful guide to the identification of this autumnal mushroom is its alternative name of 'Lawyer's Wig'. The mushroom looks exactly like something M'Lud might wear on his or her head. Sometimes found singly, but more often in colonies, Shaggy Ink Caps grow to about 20cm in height on lawns, waysides and disturbed ground.

They deliquesce as they age in a phantasmagoric manner, inverting and turning black. The 'ink' they drop from the edges of the cap is said to have been used for writing.

Cut them when young, slice and fry. They are slight in flavour, sensuous in texture. They will not preserve. You see them, you eat them. Use in any mixed mushroom recipe, such as wild mushroom soup or wild mushroom risotto.

Shaggy Ink Caps live on lawns, verges and disturbed ground.

WILD MUSHROOM SAUCE

Serves 4

This is a good recipe for mushrooms that tend to lose shape in cooking and emit a lot of discolouring 'ink'. Such as Shaggy Ink Caps. Serve over meat steaks, or just pour over pasta.

30g unsalted butter
1 tbsp extra virgin olive oil
2 shallots, finely chopped
1 clove garlic, crushed
500g Shaggy Ink Caps (or any edible mushrooms
  you can harvest), roughly chopped
salt and pepper to taste
125ml indecently good red wine
1 beef/vegetarian stock cube dissolved in 125ml water
1 sprig fresh Thyme, stripped
2 tsp chopped fresh chives
200ml cream

Heat the butter and olive oil in a frying pan over a medium heat. Add the shallots and garlic, and sauté for 2 minutes to soften. Stir in the mushrooms and season. After a few minutes add the red wine, beef stock and stripped Thyme leaves. Let the liquid cook down by about two thirds, stirring regularly to prevent burning. Take off the heat, stir in the chives and cream. Check the seasoning. Serve.

SNAILS   *Helix pomatia/Helix aspera*
Season: March–October

Think of them as Escargots, break out the claret, put Johnny Halliday on the CD player . . . and you are already more than half way to overcoming the revulsion these creatures engender as foodstuff.

In truth, there is nothing particularly French about eating Snails; they were a popular dish for Bristol's tobacco workers until the 1940s, and could be bought ready cooked from shops, in much the way London's East Enders purchased their favoured nosh of jellied eels from stalls. The Romans regarded Snails as basic fodder.

The official 'Edible Snail' (*Helix pomatia*) is commonest in the south and west of Britain, which adds weight to the theory that it was introduced by the Romans. The shell is creamy white going on brown, usually with smudgy brown bands. Since it requires undisturbed loose ground to bury in for hibernation and egg-laying it is more a creature of wasteland (and pastureland and heath) than the garden. In England, but not the rest of the UK, the Edible Snail is a protected species, and off the menu.

There are no such restrictions on the eating of the Garden Snail (*Helix aspera*), which is smaller than its cousin mollusc, and a darker brown in colour, with yellowish hoops. Both species of Snail are vegetarian.

Finding Snails is child's play, so send children, if you have any handy, out with a bucket. Snails hide under stones, rotting vegetation, and cracks in walls. Alternatively, lay some large leaves, such as those from cabbage or rhubarb, on the ground in the evening, and you will find in the morning that the Snails have come to you.

Since Snails involuntarily ingest toxins when grazing, whether man-made (pesticides, herbicides) or naturally occurring (from poisonous plants, such as deadly nightshades), they need to be purged before consumption. Place 20–30 Snails in a large metal bucket with a saucer of water, and a handful of **Dandelion** or lettuce leaves, plus **Wild Garlic** or dill leaves. Tie a piece of muslin or net curtain over the top to prevent great escapes. The herbage feeds and flavours the Snails, but you will need to clean them out every day, and replace the water and fodder. Do this for at least five days, and on two or three occasions run the Snails under the garden hose; this makes them evacuate their bowels.

ESCARGOTS DE BOURGOGNE

Serves 4

This is the French way of serving up Snails, but the preparation is applicable to any Snail dish you might fancy.

To cook: plunge the Snails into slightly salted boiling water. Bring back to the boil for 3 minutes. Remove from the shells, cut off the tortillion if you choose to (the last bit out of the shell), and rinse in clean water. Then simmer for 60–90 minutes in 'court bouillon'. Essentially this flavoured cooking liquid is one part white wine to 2 parts water, with any and every herb and vegetable that takes your fancy, although classic court bouillon consists of carrots, garlic, salt, onion, celery and pepper. If you are intending to use the shells as serving receptacles, boil them for at least 20 minutes.

For the 'Bourgogne' finish, you will need:
90g parsley
35g shallots
100g garlic
200g butter
5g salt
5g black pepper
40 cooked Escargots

Finely chop the parsley, shallots, garlic, then mix them into the butter, seasoning with the salt and pepper. Poke a little of the butter mixture into the shell, then push in a cooked Snail, and fill the rest of the shell with more of the butter. Place in a warm oven just long enough to slightly melt the butter.

Snails are an *hors d'oeuvre*, and need to be picked out of their shell with a fork. If you find them gristly, and many people do, swallow whole like Oysters. Serve with brown bread and butter.

STINGING NETTLE   *Urtica dioica*
Local Names: DEVIL'S LEAF, HEG-BEG, DEVIL'S LEAF
Season: March–May

Aside from eating your first foraged fungi, nothing you do with wild food will cause you as much trepidation as eating your first Stinging Nettles.

The underside of the Nettle leaf contains thousands of minute hypodermic syringes, and it is these that puncture the human skin to 'inject' formic acid and cause the sting that gives the plant its name. Urtica is from the Latin, *urere*, 'to burn'. In cooking, however, the syringes and formic acid are destroyed, leaving a green vegetable with an earthy flavour reminiscent of slightly bitter spinach. Steaming for 4–5 minutes is best, with the Nettles served up with a knob of butter and squirt of lemon. Like spinach, Nettles 'cook down', so gather them by the plastic bag full.

The Stinging Nettle is almost too well-known to need description. The long stem, up to over 1m in height, with bristly heart-shaped leaves, is imprinted from childhood in the mind of almost everyone as a plant to avoid. The stems bear greenish flowers in summer. Of course, a failsafe method of identification is to touch the plant.

Stinging Nettles are to be found in gardens, waste ground, woodland edges and fields. Lovers of nitrogen and phosphate, they grow best on fertile soils, which explains their particular near impenetrable abundance in farmyards and abandoned houses, notably near the former lavatory. Archaeologists even use the presence of Nettles as an indicator of sometime human habitation.

Only the young leaves at the top of the plant are to be eaten, partly because they are the tenderest, partly because the plant is a rich refuge for insects, especially the peacock and small tortoiseshell butterflies. Wear thick rubber gloves and pick the topmost leaves, as though you were picking tea leaves in Ceylon. Nettles appear in the spring and can be harvested until July. You can steal an advance on nature, as did Andrew Fairservice, the gardener in Walter Scott's *Rob Roy*, by raising them under glass. After July the leaves fill with crystals of calcium carbonate which make them grittily unpleasant.

There is more to be done with Nettles than simply serving up as a jade green veg. (If you do boil or steam them as green veg, keep the juice as soup stock.) Nettle pudding is the oldest known dish of the British. Researchers from the University of Wales Institute have found traces of Nettle pudding 8,000 years old; the Neolithic chefs blended the Nettles with barley flour, other greens, salt and water to make a dumpling to go into stews. Nettles, with help from chopped spring onions, cream, nutmeg and Parmesan cheese make an excellent quiche. They can be made into an emerald green pesto, and they combine well with strong salty cheeses such Feta. Nettle tea (dry the leaves in the sun on a sheet, then crush) is a well-known tonic: hawkers on Victorian streets used to cry: 'Nettles with tender shoots to cleanse the blood.' Certainly, Nettles have a high vitamin C and A content, and are a good source of iron, calcium, and protein. Try the Nettle tea with **Water Mint**. According to the Stuart scholar and gardener John Evelyn, consuming Nettles did more than improve the body. Writing in 1699, Evelyn observed that the 'frugal Italians and French' ate Nettle tops and considered that his countrymen should follow suit, because eating such 'Sallet' made men's conversations 'pleasant and agreeable', in contrast to the bawdy banter of the average beef-eating Englishman. Nettles were a civilising force.

In Scotland, the natives made cloth from Nettles as late as the eighteenth century (the linguistic roots of Nettle are actually from words meaning 'twist and 'cloth'). They also added Nettles to porridge, and Fife miners flagellated themselves with Nettles to cure rheumatism.

And still the list of useful things that Nettles can do goes on. Nettle juice rubbed on the pate is recommended as a cure for baldness. Indeed, many of the best uses of Nettles come in liquid form. Nettles also make a rather convincing beer, soup and purée.

NETTLE BEER

Nettle beer is a refreshing and mildly alcoholic drink, made commercially on the Continent, and simplicity itself to make in your kitchen.

**2kg (4 carrier bags full) of washed young
   Stinging Nettle leaves
30g Ground Ivy (see page 61)
9 litres water
Juice of 2 lemons
3kg white sugar
100g cream of tartar
brewer's yeast**

Equipment (sterilised before use)
**fermentation bin
muslin
airlock and bung
funnel
siphoning tube
bottles**

Boil the Nettle tips and Ground Ivy in the water for 15 minutes. Allow to cool slightly, before straining the dark brown liquid into a sterilised fermentation bin. Add the lemon juice, sugar, cream of tartar and stir well.

When the liquid is at room temperature, sprinkle the yeast on top, and cover with a layer of muslin or net curtain, tied so the material does not dip down into the liquid. After twenty four hours remove the muslin, and fit an airlock. Leave for a further five days. Strain into sterile wine bottles and cork loosely. Or you can use old plastic mineral water bottles. Store in a cool dark place for a week. Serve chilled.

NETTLE SOUP

Serves 6

Essentially, any soup made from Nettle tips, plus an onion, a potato, and a cube of vegetable stock will pass muster. This is a luxury version, which can also be used as the model for other 'Wild Green' soups such as those made from **Chickweed** and **Fat Hen**:

300g Nettle tips (about a carrier bag full)
70g unsalted butter
1 medium onion, chopped
2 cloves garlic, chopped
1 large potato, cubed
2 litres vegetable/chicken stock
6 heaped tbsp crème fraiche
1 small bunch chives, chopped for garnish
salt and pepper

Wash the Nettles (with gloves on) and discard any stalks. Melt the butter in a large saucepan over a medium heat and add the onion and garlic and sweat for 5 minutes, stirring occasionally. Add the potato and soften for a minute. Pour in the stock, bring to the boil and simmer for 5 minutes, or until the potato cubes can be mashed easily against the side of the pan. Add the Nettles and simmer for a further 5 minutes.

Cool slightly, then purée in batches. Return the soup to the pan and reheat, taking care not to boil, seasoning to taste.

Ladle the soup into bowls. Dollop in the crème fraiche, with a sprinkling of chives and season.

This soup can be served cold. It also freezes well.

NETTLE PURÉE

1kg Nettle tops
60ml boiling water
1 small onion, chopped
20 kg butter
sea salt
white pepper
pinch nutmeg

Wearing rubber gloves, wash the Nettles but don't shake dry. Put into a pan, add the boiling water and onion and simmer until wilted, about 3–5 minutes. Add the butter and seasoning, and continue to simmer for a further minute or two, stirring continuously with a wooden spoon. Purée in a liquidiser. Serve spread on toast like Laverbread, with a poached egg on top.

'Sirgan' is a version of Nettle purée from the Black Sea, which cooks the Nettles for longer in a greater amount of water, with the thickening provided by cornflour. Garlic is essential to the recipe.

ROSEBAY WILLOWHERB
Epilobium angustifolium
Local Names: FIREWEED, FRENCH WILLOW, LOOSESTRIFE, LONDON WEED
Season: April–June

Once rare, Rosebay Willowherb became a fixture in cities after World War II since it thrived on the disturbed earth of bombsites. The upright perennial, reaching 2m tall with a scarlet spike of flowers, is common on other churned ground; its country name of fireweed recognises its ability to spring from the ashes of earth devastated by forest blazes. It's also found on wasteland, riverbanks, and mountainsides.

Steam young shoots like asparagus, and use the pointed leaves as a salad/green vegetable. In Russia, the leaves are dried for tea. The mature, summertime plant is extremely bitter. In autumn, when the plant has died back, the roots can be scrubbed and scraped to release the inner pith for a potato-type mash – if you have time.

5

THE HEDGEROW

ALEXANDERS   *Smyrnium olusatrum*
Local Names: HELLROOT, SKEET, ASHINDER, HORSE PARSLEY
Season: April–November

Alexanders the Great? Imported by the Romans, Alexanders was used as a winter and spring vegetable until the eighteenth century, then it was neglected, but is now served up in all the best restaurants.

Alexanders grows in belt-high clumps. It likes roadsides, the sandy soil of the seaside, and ruins. By reputation, the plant is a marker of abandoned monasteries, for monks grew it as a salad herb. Unsurprisingly, given its Mediterranean heritage, it becomes less and less common the further north you go. The leaves are shiny, dark green, three-lobed, with serrated edges. The flowers are dense yellow umbels. Alexanders' scientific name alludes to its myrrh-like aroma.

Its position in the British kitchen was taken by a usurper, celery. As with celery, the main edible part of Alexanders is the stem. To cook Alexanders' stems: strip off the leaves and cut the now naked stalks into lengths of 8–10cm. Sauté in butter and oil until tender. Alternatively, steam for 5 minutes. Do anything with Alexanders stalks you would with celery or asparagus, though Alexanders is more intensely flavoured than both. It makes distinguished fillings for vol-au-vents, if boiled, chopped and mixed with a touch of béchamel sauce. The aromatic leaves can be used for the flavouring of fish and meat dishes, or added to salads; like the stalk, the leaves are rich in vitamin C, and were used in remedies for scurvy in the past. The florets, which appear in late spring and look for all the world like yellow calabrese, can be steamed or frittered.

In medieval times, the Irish put Alexanders, **Watercress** and **Stinging Nettles** in a soup, 'lenten pottage'. Parkinson in his *Theatricum Botanicum*, 1640, says

Our Allisanders are much used to make broth with the upper part of the roote, which is the tenderest part, and the leaves being boiled together, and some eate them raw with some vinegar, or stew them, and so eate them, and this chiefly in the time of Lent, to help digest the crudities and viscous humours [that] are gathered in the stomacke by the much use of fish at that time.

The root can be consumed too. Scrub well and roast. The taste is somewhere between parsnip and Jerusalem artichoke.

Beware of confusing Alexanders with Hemlock Water Dropwort, which has similar leaves. If in doubt wait until the flowers appear. The umbels of the poisonous Hemlock Water Dropwort are white.

In case you were wondering, Alexanders *is* named after Alexander the Great. Or perhaps, the city of Alexandria.

BALM *Melissa officinalis*
Local Names: LEMON BALM, BEE BALM
Season: May–July

Another perennial herb that long ago did a bunk over the garden wall, Balm is to be found on waysides, and near the remains of old settlements.

Up to 60cm tall, erect and with toothed nettle-like leaves, Balm is unremarkable in looks. Its beauty is below the skin. When the leaves of Balm are bruised they emit an enticing scent of lemon; this aroma of citron is the surest guide to identifying the plant.

The herb tastes of lemon too, and can be used to flavour summer drinks. Add crushed leaves to May-cup, claret-cup and chilled wine. Balm is a constituent ingredient of the liquors Chartreuse and Benedict, and makes a tea (from either dried or fresh leaves) that is fabled as an elixir. *The London Dispensary* declared in 1696: 'Balm given every morning will renew youth, strengthen the brain and relieve languishing Nature.' Presumably the good book had Prince Llewellyn of Glamorgan in mind. He reputedly drank Balm tea every morning, and lived to be 108.

Young leaves can be chopped into salads, mayonnaise, and white sauce for fish. The mature leaves of late summer are the most potent, so are the best to preserve (a process which ineluctably reduces scent and flavour). Bottle in vinegar, or dry by spreading the leaves on a tray in a sunny, draught-free position such as a windowsill. Dried Balm will enhance salmon, white fish, chicken and pork.

Early botanists labelled Balm *melissophyllum*, meaning 'Bee Leaf' because wherever the plant was to be found so were bees. Canny medieval apiarists planted Balm by the hive so that their bees would come home.

BLACKBERRY   *Rubus fruticosus*
Local Names: BRAMBLE, SCALDBERRY, BUMBLEKITE, WAIT-A-BIT
Season: August–September

A Blackberrying expedition has always been a good excuse for a family foraging expedition; the Blackberry has been part of the British diet since Neolithic times. The Blackberry (or Bramble) is not only useful for its fruits, however; the plant is heavy with cosmetic, medicinal, folkloric and religious associations. The Romans used the berries as hair dye, and the leaves as a cure for gout, and infusions of leaves continue to be staple alternative treatments for relief from diarrhoea. In the Old Testament the Bramble was chosen to rule the kingdom of the flora, and it is sometimes suggested that the plant's tendrils formed the Crown of Thorns on Christ's head at the crucifixion. There is a long-standing tradition that when Lucifer was cast out of Paradise he landed in a Blackberry bush; superstitious country people, consequently, do not pick Blackberries after Old Michaelmas Day, 11 October, because the Devil might be encountered. And your Blackberries will be rotting.

The rambling Blackberry hardly needs description. What it does require is someone in the foraging party to be carrying a walking stick, because the ripest, most luscious berries are always those on the thorniest stem furthest away and closest to the sun, and the curved handle of a walking stick is ideal for hoisting them down. Blackberries should be picked into punnets, small Tupperware-type boxes (lid off), or a plastic ice-cream tub because in the forager's ubiquitous hold-all, the carrier bag, they become battered and brusied.

Of course, the danger of picking Blackberries is that by the time you have tasted them, and rewarded yourself for their picking, there are not as many in the punnet as could be. Those that do make it home can be turned into wine, into cordial, into 'Bramble Jelly' (see the recipe for hedgerow fruits on page 100), and plonked on top of vanilla ice cream for the quickest pudding known. Whatever you do with your Blackberries, do it quickly because they will not keep for more than a few hours.

The unique flavour of the cooked Blackberry is, I think, not sufficiently appreciated. A pleasing take on fruit fool can be achieved by simmering 450g Blackberries with 225g sugar, thickened with a dab of cornflour and a dash of lemon juice. Served cold, very cold.

The Anglo-Saxons called the plant *bremel*, the origin of Bramble. By the Middle Ages the plant, which is a natural hybrid of two Rose species, had acquired many local names, usually recognising the difficulty of picking the fruit, including the cautionary Wait-a-bit. In some parts of Britain, it was called Scaldberry in the false belief that if children ate too freely of the berries they would develop scurf or eczema.

Over a hundred wild varieties of Blackberry exist in Britain today; the fruit is so bountiful because the rose-like flowers of the Bramble bloom from June to October and carry large supplies of easily accessible nectar which makes them attractive to insectoid pollinators.

There is only one plant that could possibly be confused with the Blackberry, and that is the equally succulent and safe-to-eat Dewberry.

BLACKBERRY WINE

Adapted from *Discovering Hedgerows* by David Street and Rosamond Richardson, 1982. This makes a light, dry red wine that is ideal with cheese and red meat.

2kg Blackberries
3.5 litres boiling water
1kg sugar
1 tsp citric acid
1 sachet wine yeast

Equipment (sterilised before use)
large bowl/stainless steel bucket/cauldron
2 x 4.5 litre demi-johns
airlock and bung
rubber bung
muslin
siphon tube
bottles

Sort, wash, then crush the fruit in a bowl. Pour in the boiling water. Cover with muslin and leave to cool. Stir in the sugar, acid and yeast. Replace the cover and allow to ferment, pressing down on the fruit twice per day.

Strain out, press dry and discard the pulp. Pour the must into a sterilised demi-john. Fit an airlock and leave in a warm room until the wine finishes fermentation and begins to clear. This should take about 2 weeks.

Siphon the wine into a sterilised jar, throw away the sediment and top up with cold boiled water. Bung tightly and leave in a cool place until the wine is bright. Siphon into bottles and store for a year.

BLACKTHORN *Prunus spinosa*
Local Names: BULLEN, SLAATHORN, SNAG, BUSH, BLACKHAW, BUCKTHORN
Season: October–November

In time gone by, farmers planted Blackthorn alongside Hawthorn in their hedges because the shrub's spines were fearsome enough to keep livestock in. So, take gardening gloves with you when you go gathering the sloe, the autumn fruit of the Blackthorn.

The globose sloe berry is about 12mm across, blue at first then going on black, sometimes with a greyish bloom. Clustered on the stem, sloes are gorgeously, bounteously inviting in late autumn – but beware, they are sharply acidic when raw. According to folklore, they sweeten after the first frosts. But lore it is, not truth. They are always tart. The fruit is chiefly known for its role in 'sloe gin', with the traditional recipe given to George Orwell by Hampshire gypsies being as good as any other.

Pick your sloes when they be fine and ripe, with dry air, and warm with the sun. Prick each one with a needle three times. Take half a bottle of unsweetened gin and put in a fistful of sugar-candy, firm and strong, the taste of a crushed bitter almond or the kernels of ripe apricots, crushed. Fill the bottle with sloes and press them down. If you be not on the road, lay beneath the floor of your tent where you be sleeping, for they slags (sloes) dunnot like the cold. Let 'em bide till Christmas come, when take out the fruit and let 'em bide till you need 'em.

The cheaper the gin, the better. Indeed, the practice of adding sloes to gin likely arose as a way of making cheap spirits palatable. If you don't feel like the tedious labour of pricking each sloe with a pin, use a fork, or if feeling lazier yet, stick the sloes in the freezer overnight and defrost, because this too will rupture the skins. The sloe gin of the Hampshire gentleman of the road would have been best if he had been a-travelling, because motion mixes the sloe gin ingredients up. So, turn your jar (with a leakproof lid) upside down once a day.

The resultant ruby red liquor improves with age.

Do not waste the mash of damson flesh left behind. Strain through muslin or net curtain, and mix 3 to 1 with sugar. Boil. And serve up as sauce for game.

Then again, if you have a sweet tooth, the leftover sloes make delicious home-made liqueur chocolates. Cut the flesh off the fruit, add to melted chocolate, then spoon onto rice paper about 2cm thick. Let it set in the fridge, then cut into squares.

In spring, Blackthorn bursts with delicate white blossom – a useful marker for future foraging reference – as though it were puffing smoke.

HEDGEROW TOFFEE APPLES
A recipe from Andy Hamilton, made for BBC's *Autumnwatch*.

50g assorted hedgerow fruit (sloes, haws, hips, etc)
150ml water
225g sugar
½ tsp red wine vinegar
2 tbsp maple syrup
25g butter
6 apples
6 fat twigs/sticks

Boil the hedgerow fruit in the water for 10 minutes until it starts to change colour. If using hips, sloes or anything that can't be mushed between your fingers easily, then freeze overnight and thaw before using.

Strain through a muslin cloth and measure 110ml of the resulting water. It should have changed to a lovely reddish/purplish colour (depending on what fruit you are using). Gently heat, stirring in the sugar until fully dissolved and adding the vinegar, syrup and butter. Bring the mixture to the boil and keep at as close to 138°C as you can for 10 minutes. You'll be able to tell when it is done by dropping a bit of the semi-solid liquid into cold water; if it turns to a ball it is done.

Pull the stalks out of the apples and whack the sticks in. Roll the apples in the semi-solid until coated and repeat. Leave to harden on grease proof paper.

BULLACE   *Prunus domestica subsp. insititia*
Local Names: BULLUM TREE, WILD PLUM, BULLISON, WILD DAMSON
Season: September–October

The Bullace is the ancestor of the cultivated Damson, and its fruit is sweeter than that of its relation, the **Blackthorn**, with whom it shares the same habitats of hedgerow, scrub and wasteland. You can eat a Bullace fruit without your mouth involuntarily puckering.

The Bullace is not native to these isles, and in truth is more feral than wild. Bullace's alternative name of Wild Damson is the clue to its origin: 'Damson' is derived from 'Damascus plum'. The fruit was first cultivated in that Syrian city and, like Ground Elder and Rabbit, like Balm and Borage, was brought to Britain by the Romans.

The blueish fruits of the Bullace, which are larger and more egg-shaped than sloes, ripen in early autumn and rot quickly. They make a port-like wine, a cordial, a syrup, and can be added to vodka to make Bullace vodka.

If any Bullace fruits survive vodka-making, or you have fruits 'on the turn', turn them into game sauce.

The fruits of three other members of the clan Prunus are also worth gathering. The Cherry Plum (*Prunus cerasifera*) is naturalised in southern England, and has late summer fruits that are just edible raw, but better made into jam; the fruits of the Wild Cherry or Gean (*Prunus avium*) used to be sold on the streets of London, and have been foraged in Britain for thousands of years; the Bird Cherry (*Prunus padus*), common in northern Britain, produced bitter near-black fruits that need sugar and stewing.

BULLACE JAM
800g Bullaces
500ml water
1.2kg sugar

Gently simmer the Bullaces in the water until the stones rise and can be skimmed off. Add the sugar and boil rapidly for about 8 minutes until the mixture reaches setting point (turn down heat, spoon a little into a saucer and see if it begins to 'set'). If it is setting, skim off any scum, wait 10 minutes for the jam to cool, then pour into sterilised, warm jars. If not setting, boil for longer.

An alternative to skimming off the scum – which inevitably results in the loss of some jam – is to stir in a knob of butter at the end of cooking. Like magic, the scum disappears.

BULLACE VODKA
225g Bullaces
50g sugar
570ml vodka

Wash the Bullaces, and remove all the stalks and leaves. Prick over with a fork. Drop into a bottle until they come to about a third of the way up. Pour in the sugar through a funnel, then pour in the vodka. Shake (with top on), and shake once daily for three months. Strain off into another bottle. Drink within six months.

Blackberry vodka can be made in the same way. Strain off the fruit after six weeks.

BULLACE CHUTNEY

Fills 6–8 x 340g jars

Chutney is a terrific and tangy way of preserving the wild food harvest – and a less nerve-wracking one than jam-making, because chutney does not need to set.

1.5kg Bullaces
400g Crab Apples
400g shallots, chopped
500ml cider vinegar
1 clove garlic, crushed
1 tsp mustard
½ tsp ground ginger
½ tsp cayenne pepper
black pepper
500g light brown sugar

Wash the Bullaces and de-stone. Peel, core and slice the apples and place in a pan. Add the chopped shallots, vinegar, crushed garlic, and spices. Simmer uncovered gently for 15 minutes. Add the Bullaces and sugar. Turn up the heat and simmer until the mixture thickens and goes glossy, about another 30 minutes. Stir regularly to prevent burning. Spoon into sterile jars while warm, and push down with a spoon to remove air pockets. Seal and leave in a cool, dark place to mature for at least two months. Use within 18 months.

COMMON MALLOW   *Malva sylvestris*

Local Names: HIGH MALLOW, BREAD-AND-CHEESE, MALLACE, RAGS AND TATTERS, CHEESE FLOWER, BUTTER AND CHEESE, CHEESE CAKE FLOWERS, LADY'S CHEESE, TRUCKLES OF CHEESE

Season: April–June (leaves), July–October (flowers)

This big perennial herb puts on quite a roadside show in late summer with its pink, bling flowers stretching to 4cm across. They make an eye-catching decoration in a salad. The plant is widespread across Britain, though commonest in Essex, the South, the centre of England, and Wales.

Before the flowers do their unsubtle act, the mucilaginous leaves can be picked and chopped, then eaten raw or cooked. The Tudor herbalist John Gerard was firmly of the opinion that *Malva sylvestris* had no place in the garden; after you have munched the leaves you may well agree. A pleasant enough flavour, but heavy masticating is needed. The thing to look out for on the wayside Mallow is the seed disk, which looks exactly like a pale green wheel of cheese, hence the multiplicity of 'cheesy' folk names for the plant. Moist and crisp, the disks make a pleasing nibble, tasting something like peanuts.

All the *Malva* family which live in Britain have edible leaves, flowers and seed pods, and historically all have been prized by apothecaries, herbalists and practitioners of herbal medicine. Back in Ancient Rome, Pliny opined that a mere spoonful of Mallow a day would keep the physician away. For centuries after, Mallow was gathered to make poultices and lotions. And laxatives.

The chewy confectionery 'Marsh Mallow' was originally made from Common Mallow's rare kin, the Marsh Mallow, whose root contains an especially glutinous syrup. (Today's spongy cubes, almost wholly made from sugar, share only the name with the traditional recipe.) Found on coastal tracts, especially in the southern half of the country, Marsh Mallow's autumn roots can profitably be softened by boiling, then shallow fried. On the other hand, you could do what Pliny did when not extolling Mallow's medicinal virtues: stuff a suckling pig with it.

COW PARSLEY   *Anthriscus sylvestris*

Local Names: DEVIL'S MEAL, DEVIL'S MEAT, COW-MUMBLE, QUEEN ANNE'S LACE, KEX, ADDER'S MEAT, GIPSY CURTAINS, HARE'S PARSLEY, WILD CHERVIL, DOG PARSLEY, COW WEED.
Season: March–June

This common herb whitens the roadsides and hedgerows in June with billowing clouds of lacey flowers. Long before then, as early as January in the south of England, the delicate fern-like leaves have 'greened up' the same waysides; it is these young tender leaves, with their mild notes of aniseed and myrrh, that are useful in flavouring salads, omelettes, and, above all, fish dishes, by chopping in raw and generously. Always add towards the end of cooking to avoid flavour loss. The leaves will bear drying, but the process does lessen flavour. The cultivated relative of Cow Parsley, Chervil (*Anthriscus cerefolium*) is regarded by the French as one of the traditional *fines herbes*.

Herbalists of old attached miraculous medicinal powers to Cow Parsley, believing it protected against everything from chills to plague. The root was the main part of the plant used in medicinal preparations. John Gerard recommended it in 1597 for old people 'that are dull and without courage; it rejoiceth and comforteth the heart, and increaseth their strength'.

A pretty and useful herb though Cow Parsley is, it has a connection with the Devil ('Devil's Meat') for good reason. It can be confused with several other species, notably the ultra poisonous Hemlock (*Conium maculatum*), the plant Socrates used for his suicide. Cow Parsley also has a more than a passing resemblance to the poisonous Fool's Parsley (*Aethusa cynapium*). You have to be absolutely sure you are picking Cow Parsley, and not some deadly impostor: the main difference between Cow Parsley and Hemlock and Fool's Parsley is that the stem of Cow Parsley is furrowed and slightly hairy. The stem of Hemlock is smooth and spotted with purple, and smells foul; the stem of Fool's Parsley is thin and hairless. But use a good guidebook, or get an expert to identify. **If in doubt, do not pick**.

PAPILLOTES OF SALMON WITH COW PARSLEY

Serves 4

Adapted from *Cooking with Herbs*, Patricia Lousada, 1988.

3 tbsp finely chopped Cow Parsley leaves
30g butter
salt and pepper
oil
4 thick salmon steaks

Mash the Cow Parsley into the butter, and season with salt and pepper. Put on a side plate, pat into a bar shape, and refrigerate until firm.

Cut four squares from aluminium foil big enough to contain a fish steak when folded in half. Oil one half of the foil and place a steak on it. Cut off a quarter of the butter bar, place on top of the fish and seal by folding over the foil and crimping the edges. The parcel should be tightly sealed but roomy. Preheat the oven to 200°C/Gas Mark 6. Bake the parcels for 10–12 minutes.

DEAD NETTLES
Lamium album/Lamium purpureum

Local Names: (White Dead-Nettle) SUCKY SUE, HELMET FLOWER, BEE-NETTLE, ADAM-AND-EVE-IN-THE-BOWER, WHITE ARCHANGEL; (Red Dead-Nettle) BAD MAN'S POSIES, BUMBLEBEE-FLOWER, ARCHANGEL, DUMB NETTLE, DEE NETTLE

Season: March–May

Neither White Dead-Nettle (*Lamium album*) nor Red Dead-Nettle (*Lamium purpureum*) sting, both are edible, both like wasteland and hedgerows.

White Dead-Nettle is a hairy perennial, common throughout Britain, except the south; the flowers are white, with a hooded upper lip. Geoffrey Grigson notes in *The*

Englishman's Flora, 'turn the plant upside down, and beneath the white upper lip of the corolla, Adam and Eve, the black and gold stamens, lie side by side, like two human figures'. Its local names include Adam-and-Eve-in-the-Bower.

Pick the young leaves and shoots before flowering to eat in green salad, or cook like spinach.

The leaves of Red Dead-Nettle (*Lamium purpureum*) have a pungent scent when crushed; they make good greens. The pinkish-purple flowers can be candied in the manner of **Sweet Violet**.

GARLIC MUSTARD *Alliaria petiolata*
Local Names: GARLIC ROOT, SAUCE ALONE, HEDGE GARLIC, PENNY HEDGE, POOR MAN'S MUSTARD, JACK-BY-THE-HEDGE
Season: March–April (leaves)
October–December (roots)

Garlic Mustard is a familiar of roadside verges, thus its country name of 'Jack-by-the-hedge'. It bursts forth in early spring to stand tall and soldier-straight, bearing light green leaves and later clusters of white flowers from the top of the stem. But the easiest method of identifying the plant is to crush one of the heart-shaped leaves: a distinct garlicky aroma is released.

Culpeper sagely advised in his *Herbal* apropos of Garlic Mustard, 'Reader, just try a little in your next salad.' The garlic tang of leaves does make a sensational addition to green salad, although they wilt with alarming rapidity so use quickly. Snip a leaf or two from each plant, rather than stripping a plant naked. Historically, the green leaves were used as a sauce for mutton and fish, a basic version being to take two handfuls of Hedge Garlic leaves, one Mint leaf, tear, mash into 2 tablespoons of vinegar, and a touch of sugar to personal taste.

Garlic Mustard leaves are best just before the plant flowers, but if you don't catch it before then, it's still good. The flowers are edible too. They have four small white petals, in the shape of a cross, revealing Garlic Mustard's membership of the large crucifer family (kale, cabbage, *et al*).

When summer is a memory, and the Garlic Mustard has turned into a brown skeleton, dig up a specimen or three, and grate and pound the slender white taproots. With the addition of a little oil and vinegar a perfectly passable alternative for **Horseradish** sauce is yours. Likewise, the black seeds hanging in the near transparent flat pods can be ground into a mustard substitute.

This highly invasive biennial is to be found across Britain, with the exception of the far north of Scotland. Look for it on wasteland, as well as countryside lanes.

GARLIC MUSTARD PESTO
100g Garlic Mustard leaves
1 clove garlic
50g pine nuts
5 gherkins
50g grated Parmesan
10 tbsp oil
salt and pepper

Wash, shake and roughly chop the leaves. Put them in the blender with the garlic, pine nuts, gherkins and blend until a smooth paste is achieved. Add the Parmesan, oil, pinch of salt, and dash of pepper. Give the blender a short burst.

GROUND IVY *Glechoma hederacea*
Local Names: ALEHOOF, GILL-OVER-THE-GROUND, GILL-BY-THE-GROUND, TUNHOOF, HEDGE-MAIDS, HAY-MAIDENS, JENNY-RUN-BY-THE-GROUND, LIZZY-RUN-UP-THE-HEDGE
Season: March–May

Ground Ivy is a shy creeping plant, growing in carpets in the shadowed base of hedges and walls. The leaves are roundish, crenated, hairy, and sometimes purplish underneath. In summer it bears tubular violet flowers.

Three of Ground Ivy's local names, Alehoof, Gill-over-the-ground (from the French 'guiller', to ferment) and Tunhoof, are relics of its role in the brewing industry from Saxon times until its supersession by **Hops** in the sixteenth century. Ground Ivy was used to clarify and flavour, and to preserve beer on sea voyages. And a crushed leaf will instantly inform you why Ground Ivy was prescribed by 'physicks' for catarrh: a harsh menthol vapour is released. Catarrh was only one of numerous complaints apothecaries believed Ground Ivy could cure, whether by syrup, tea ('gill tea'), infusion or snuff. As far back as the second century AD Galen noted the use of Ground Ivy for treating inflamed eyes. The plant has also been used to treat diseases of the lungs, bladder, kidneys and brain.

Ground Ivy is a relative of Mint, Lavender and Sage. Used in small amounts in spring, Ground Ivy makes an interesting addition to salad, and at a desperate pinch it can be used as a green vegetable. In medieval times it was made into a stuffing for pork.

For reasons now lost, Ground Ivy was associated with girls, as well as beer and cough-cures. 'Gill' itself was a play on the maid's name 'Jill', while the feminine connection is clearly seen in the local names Hay-Maids, Lizzy-run-up-the-hedge, Jenny-run-by-the-ground.

Ground Ivy has an unusual botanical feature; some individual plants possess large and small flowers, the large flowers being hermaphrodite – meaning they possess both the female style and stigma and the male stamens – and the smaller flowers are female only. The arrangement increases the chances of cross-pollination.

HERB BEER

In his *Health from Wild British Herbs*, 1918, Richard Lawrence Hook gives a recipe for a herb beer in which Ground Ivy is a principal ingredient:

Ground Ivy 2 oz [60g]
Wood Sage 1 oz [30g]
Yellow Dock Root 1 oz [30g]
Dandelion Root 1 oz [30g]
Burdock Root 2 oz [60g]
Stinging Nettle Root 1 oz [30g]
Sassafras Chips 1 oz [30g]
Ginger, crushed 4 oz [120g]

The whole to be gently boiled for half an hour in 8 gallons [36.36 litres] of water. Strain into an earthenware pan containing 3 lb [1.3kg] of best black treacle or West Indian molasses; let it cool down to about 75°F [24°C], then add 1 oz [30g] of fresh German yeast (be sure the yeast is fresh) or two-thirds of a pint [0.3 litre] of brewer's barm; let it stand for 4 hours; skim the top and add 8 oz [250g] of fine, white sugar. Stir it well, and bottle for use. This makes an excellent beverage, containing splendid tonic and blood-purifying properties.

HOGWEED   *Heracleum sphondylium*
Local Names: COW PARSNIP, COW BELLY, BROAD KEX, PIG'S FLOP, PIGWEED, HUMPERSCRUMP
Season: April–June

Hogweed is much prized by foragers for its young shoots which, when boiled in salted water, taste like asparagus. I hesitate to recommend this 'Poor Man's Asparagus', however, because of its similarity to Giant Hogweed (*H. mantegazzianum*), which contains a powerful blistering agent in its sap. Giant Hogweed lives up to its name, growing up to 5m in height, whereas Hogweed reaches only 1.5 m.

Beware too, Hogweed's more than passing resemblance to Hemlock (*Conium maculatum*), which is drop dead dangerous. And beware too, that Hogweed also contains the same blistering agent as Giant Hogweed, albeit in lesser degree – enough though to affect some people.

That said, Hogweed is alleged to have healing properties which were discovered by Heracles, the Greek hero – hence its Latin name 'Heracleum'. In herbal medicine the seeds were boiled in oil to cure sores and shingles. Culpeper recommended a decoction of the seeds applied to the ear for earache. In homeopathy, potencies of *Heracleum sphondylium* are used to treat maladies of the head and stomach.

Dried leaf stalks are a culinary delicacy in Russia. The plant is rich in vitamin C and carbohydrate. Until recently, it was gathered by cottagers across Europe not just for home cooking but for foddering livestock. The plant's popular name in Britain refers both to its role as pig food but also to its unpleasant smell. Not all wild flowers smell sweet like honeysuckle to lure pollinators; Hogweed has evolved the opposite strategy for attracting flies, of stinking like a hog.

HAWTHORN   *Crataegus monogyna*
Local Names: MAY-BUSH, MAY, WHITETHORN, BREAD AND CHEESE TREE, AZZY TREE, FAIRY THORN
Season: March–April (leaves)
September–October (berries)

The flowering of the 'May' is one of the quintessential sights of Britain in early summer. Up close, the dense heavily clusters of white flowers are heavily scented. The blooms of the Hawthorn appear some weeks after the emergence of the shiny dark, much lobed leaves.

The Hawthorn, if left to its own devices, will grow into a small tree of about 10m in height, but is usually curtailed; Hawthorn has been planted deliberately in country hedgerows for centuries by farmers, because its thorns make boundaries 'stock proof'.

Until the 1950s, young children walking to school in the countryside would munch new Hawthorn leaves and shoots as a wayside nibble, called in many places 'Bread-and-Cheese'. This is a misnomer; the flavour of the young leaves is nutty and acrid. Try adding to spring salads, using as garnish.

The dark red berries which follow the flowers are more palatable. Between 7–14mm long, the 'haws' of autumn have a single pip, are rich in vitamin C and have a taste vaguely reminiscent of avocado. Traditionally they are cooked to make a jelly to accompany meat, or steeped in hot water for a herbal tea said to be a tonic for the heart. This may well be true: Hawthorn is a member of the Rose family, and in Europe Hawthorn juice is marketed as being beneficial to sufferers from hypertension and cardiovascular disease following the clinical discovery that elements in Hawthorn widen blood vessels.

There is another native Hawthorn, the Midland Hawthorn (*C. laevigata*), which is chiefly a woodland shrub. Its leaves and fruits are also edible.

There is a great deal of popular folklore attached to the Hawthorn. It has long been regarded as unlucky to bring Hawthorn blossom into the house because it would cause death in the family; on the other hand, the plant has several Christian superstitions; it was believed that Hawthorn picked on Maundy Thursday would stop the picker's house from being struck by lightning. At Glastonbury there is a Hawthorn tree said to have sprouted from the staff of Joseph of Arimathea; the miraculous thorn grew, always blossoming on Christmas Day. More profanely, girls used to bathe their faces in Hawthorn dew on May Day morning in the belief that it would make them beautiful:

The fair maid who the first of May
Goes to the field at the break of day
And washes in dew from the hawthorn tree
Will ever after handsome be

The Hawthorn is also reputed to divine bad weather. 'Many haws, many snaws,' runs the old wives' tale. This piece of folkloric forecasting flounders on the abundance of Hawthorn haws every year. But you do have to beat the birds to them, especially the migrating thrush family.

HAWTHORN JELLY
Adapted from Jason Hill's *Wild Foods of Britain*, 1939.

Pick and de-stalk the Hawthorn fruit (haws) by rubbing them between your palms. Wash the haws then simmer in a heavy saucepan with a handful of Crab Apples, reckoning that 450g fruit requires 300ml water as covering. This will take between 30–45 minutes. Mash with a potato masher, then strain the liquid through a jelly bag overnight. To the collected juice add sugar at the rate of 225g for every 600ml of liquid, plus a generous squeeze of lemon juice. Bring to the boil, stirring continuously until the sugar is dissolved. Continue boiling for 10 minutes, then pour into warmed, sterilised jars, and screw on lid. The Hawthorn jelly will keep for several months in a cool, dark place.

HOP   *Humulus lupulus*
Local Name: GREEN BINDWEED
Season: April (shoots), July–September (cones)

Although the Hop is native to Britain, the plant climbing wild in hedges and up telegraph poles is almost certainly a descendant of escapees from the Hop gardens of Kent and Herefordshire. Commercial varieties of Hop were introduced into Britain in the early sixteenth century by Flemish immigrants who were wise to the excellence of Hop's female catkins (the distinctive aromatic cones) in the brewing of beer. To dry the cones commercially these were spread on the upper floors of an oast house or Hop kiln, with a fire below. You can get the same effect by stringing up bines of Hop in the ceiling of a room or the top of the stairs, but avoid direct sunlight because this degrades lupulin, the yellow resinous powder in the cone that produces bitterness.

Somnambulists rightly swear by a pillow of Hop cones under the head (lupulin is also a calming agent; the plant is from the same botanical family as cannabis), or the drinking of Hop tea. To make: simply pour boiling water on a handful of dried Hops.

Anyone in want of a square meal should cut the young Hop shoots which appear in the spring. According to Pliny, the shoots were eaten in Ancient Rome as both vegetable and salad, and they are still widely eaten across Europe. In France *jets de houblon* are eaten as if they were thin asparagus, steamed and dipped in Hollandaise sauce or butter. The Italians sauté *punte di luppolo* with garlic, and the Belgians coat the shoots with egg sauces.

The scientific name for Hop comes from *hummus*, earth, and *lupus*, wolf, the latter referring to the plant's habit of attacking and strangling its host. The English name is altogether more prosaic, and comes from the Anglo-Saxon *hoppan*, meaning to climb.

Beware that young Hop shoots look like Black and White Bryony, which is poisonous. The aroma of Hop is distinctive, however, even in the shoots.

HOP OMELETTE

Serves 4

Hops have an affinity for hen's eggs.

200g Hop shoots
4 tbsp extra virgin olive oil
6 large eggs
25g grated Parmesan cheese
pinch chervil
salt and pepper

Wash the Hop shoots and drain. Pour the oil into a non-stick saucepan and heat. Fry the Hop shoots gently until they 'wilt'. Beat the eggs with a fork, add the Parmesan cheese, chervil and salt and pepper. Pour into the frying pan, and turn up the heat slightly until the bottom of the omelette is golden brown. Put a plate on top of the pan, and invert. Slide the omelette back into the pan, moist side down, and fry this side.

Serve hot or, better still, cold, in wedges, with green salad.

Hop shoots also make toothsome fritters. Dip into a batter, deep fry until golden. Drain on kitchen towel, and serve sprinkled with sea salt.

HOP BEER

This fail-safe recipe is from Andy Hamilton's *Booze for Free*.

13 litres water
1kg malt extract
750g sugar
55g dried Hops
ale yeast

Equipment (sterilised before use)
large saucepan
muslin
large wooden spoon
fermentation bin
hydrometer
thermometer
siphoning tube
bottles

Bring half the water to the boil, pour in the malt extract and sugar, and continue on a rolling boil for 30 minutes with the occasional stir. Put in the Hops, and continue to boil for another 30 minutes.

Strain the liquor into the fermentation bin. Pour over the rest of the water (cold) and when the temperature reaches 18°C sprinkle on the yeast. If you are using a hydrometer, the gravity should be approximately 1030.

Seal the bin and leave for a week or until it has fermented.

Place a level teaspoon of sugar into each empty beer bottle and siphon in the liquid, taking care not to drag in any sediment. Cap.

Leave the bottles for ten days. The beer should be about 4.4% alcohol.

If so desired, you can flavour the alcohol with herbs, such as **Ground Ivy** and **Yarrow**, both of which will make bitter bitterer.

HORSERADISH *Armoracia rusticana*
Local Name: RED COLE
Season: September–March

Long ago Horseradish was cultivated as a medicinal herb, but in the sixteenth century the Germans began employing it as flavouring in fish sauces. The culinary use of Horseradish spread westwards to Britain, where the sharp pungency of the plant was discovered to be ideal for the national dish, roast beef.

The 'heat' in Horseradish comes from a volatile oil, sinigrin, which is present throughout the plant. The large feathery leaves (which can reach 1m) emit a pungent aroma when crushed (a useful clue in identification) and can, when very young, be added to salads. But it is the grated white flesh of the long, long root that is used in Horseradish sauce.

Try the sauce with oily fish as well as beef. It can also be grated into coleslaw and cream cheese. The First World War forager T. Cameron, who was clearly made of tough stuff, suggested that 'the root may be cut across in thin slices and eaten as an *hors d'oeuvre* like radishes'. Fresh root contains calcium, magnesium, sodium, vitamin C, and has antibiotic qualities. When preparing Horseradish roots, have the kitchen windows wide open; the essential oils released from the root are eye-watering beyond anything onions can do. A gas-mask is useful.

Since the oil evaporates rapidly, Horseradish is little use in cooked dishes.

Look for Horseradish on wasteland, near old railway lines and on verges. Gather in autumn, remembering that you need the landowner's permission to dig up the roots. Store freshly-lifted roots in a bucket of dry sand and they'll keep for months. Alternatively, Horseradish freezes quite well when wrapped tightly. If you want to buy Horseradish go to a grocer's in an orthodox Jewish neighbourhood at Passover. Horseradish is one of the five herbs of the Seder, served to remind Jews of the bitterness and harshness of their captivity in Egypt.

HORSERADISH CREAM

Serves 4

A piquant sauce to accompany a brisket of beef, a shoulder of wild boar, a haunch of venison.

1 shallot, chopped
1 clove garlic, crushed
10g butter
75ml chicken stock
250ml double cream
30g freshly grated Horseradish root

Sweat the shallot and garlic in the butter, taking care not to brown. Add the stock, turn up the heat, and reduce by half. Add the cream and bring to the boil. Stir in the Horseradish and serve.

WILD ROSE/DOG ROSE   *Rosa canina*

Local Names: BRIAR-ROSE, HIP-ROSE, BRIAR, DOG BRIAR, CANKER, CANKER-ROSE, LAWYERS
Season: September–November

Rosehips, the scarlet oval fruits of the Wild or Dog Rose, are one of the superfoods of the British wild food pantry containing, pound for pound, 20 times the vitamin C of oranges. Small wonder therefore that during World War II – when importation of citrus fruits was somewhat hampered by U-boats – the Ministry of Food sent thousands of people out each autumn to harvest the fruit of the rambling Dog Rose from the nation's hedges. By 1943 around 450 tons of Rosehips were gathered annually. The official Ministry of Food recipe for Rosehip syrup from World War II is given overleaf.

I hope the wartime gatherers wore leather gloves. The 'dog' in 'Dog Rose' is actually a corruption of 'dag', meaning sharp knife, in honour of the plant's formidable thorns. At least that is the derivation of Dog Rose according to some authorities; others cite Pliny's tale of the Roman Emperor's Praetorian Guard who cured himself of rabies from a dog's bite with the plant's root.

When you have brought your Rosehips home, there is a multitude of good uses to which they can be put, once you divest the hips of the small hairy seeds packed sardine-tight inside the fruit which are an irritant to the stomach. For recipes involving hip 'flesh' split the fruit with a thumb nail and scrape out the contents. All liquid recipes will require a jelly bag, or some similar very fine straining material.

The Tudors made mead from hips. If you want something Rosehippy that is more appropriate for children, the hips can be puréed, then spread on foil and baked in the oven for a fruit 'leather' that makes a snack liked by children and a parent's conscience. Rosehips can also be turned into wholesome soups, tarts and teas, jellies and jams.

Then again, if you are of impish mind, you can give the discarded Rosehip hairs to children who can stick them down someone's neck as a prosaic itching powder.

The Wild Rose, though, is a floral contradiction, because its summer flowers, white or pink, are delicate, gentle and sweetly scented and thus utterly unlike the rufty-tufty haws. They can be used for Rose-petal jelly, Turkish delight, Elderflower champagne, ice cream, salads, and like **Sweet Violet**, they can be candied.

ROSEHIP SYRUP

This recipe is from the Ministry of Food's leaflet, 'Hedgerow Harvest', 1943. You'll need 2 lb (900g) of Rosehips and 12 oz (335g) honey.

Have ready 3 pints [1.7 litres] boiling water, mince the hips in a coarse mincer, drop immediately into the boiling water or if possible mince the hips directly into the boiling water and again bring to the boil. Stop heating and place aside for 15 minutes. Pour into a flannel or linen crash jelly bag and allow to drip until the bulk of the liquid has come through. Return the residue to the saucepan, add 1½ pints [900ml] boiling water, stir and allow to stand for 10 minutes. Pour back into the jelly bag and allow to drip. To make sure all the sharp hairs are removed, put back the first half-cupful of liquid and allow to drip through again. Put the mixed juice into a clean saucepan and boil down until the juice measures about 1½ pints [900ml], then add 1½ lb [650g] of sugar and boil for a further 5 minutes. Put into hot sterile bottles and seal at once. If corks are used these should have been boiled for half an hour just previously, and after insertion coated with melted paraffin wax. It is advisable to use small bottles as the syrup will not keep for more than a week or two once the bottle is opened. Store in a dark cupboard.

ROSEHIP TEA

Tangy, fruity and immensely good for you, Rosehip has everything going for it. Except for the fiddly preparation involved in removing the hairs from the hips.

First collect your Rosehips, as ripe as possible, then semi dry them either in the oven or in a food dehydrator. When they are wrinkly but not desiccated, split the individual hips open and scrape out the hairs. Then complete the drying process.

Alternatively, you can completely dry the hips, then blitz in a food processor until they are chopped up but not ground up. Then shake through a metal sieve; the hairs will fall through, leaving you with clean hips.

Whichever method above you use, return to the food processor and process until you have distinct, small bits.

The dried hips will keep in an airtight jar for several months.

To make tea, place 4 heaped teaspoons of dried Rosehips in a tea pot and steep in hot water for 10 minutes. Sweeten with honey if necessary, but do not add milk.

NYPONSOPPA

Serves 4

This Swedish soup, blood red in colour, is traditionally served as pudding.

600ml Rosehips
2.6 litres water
3 tbsp potato flour
100g sugar
4 tsp ground almonds

Rinse the Rosehips and place them in a heavy-bottomed saucepan with the water, and bring to the boil. Simmer, stirring occasionally, until the hips are soft (about 20–30 minutes). Blend the hip pulp in a mixer and pass through a fine sieve or jelly bag, returning the liquid to the saucepan. Stir the potato flour into a little cold water, then add to the saucepan, along with the sugar. Bring to the boil again. Turn down the heat, and let the soup cool. Serve with ground almonds on top. Macaroons and ice cream are also familiar floats in Nyponsoppa.

WILD ROSE BLOSSOM ICE CREAM

Serves 4

Any fragrant edible blossom will do, so long as it is abundant.

100ml full fat milk
200ml double cream
4 cupfuls blossom
1 tsp vanilla essence
2 egg yolks
30g caster sugar

Pour the milk and cream into a saucepan with the blossom and vanilla essence. Heat the mixture until it begins to simmer. Remove, put to one side and let steep for 30 minutes. Strain out the blossom.

Whisk the egg yolks with the sugar until creamy. Then gently pour the cream mixture onto the yolks, whisking all the while. Return the mixture to the saucepan and heat for a minute or two to thicken.

Pour into an ice-cream machine, if you have one, and churn. Otherwise, pour the ice cream into a bowl and refrigerate.

6

THE FIELD

CHAMOMILE *Chamaemelum nobile*
Local Names: CAMIL, CAMOMINE, ROMAN CHAMOMILE
Season: May–July

This is the stuff for a herbal tea to relax by. Snip off the daisy-like flowers in high summer, and immerse in boiling water at the rate of 25g of petals to 250ml water. Conveniently, the heads dry well, and can be kept in screw-topped jars for several months, ensuring a constant supply.

Also known by the Latin tag *Anthemis nobilis*, Chamomile is a creeping perennial, a variety of which was once used to make aromatic lawns, including those at Buckingham Palace. Native to southern and western Europe you will find Chamomile on dry grassland, heaths and roadsides.

FAT HEN *Chenopodium album*
Local Names: MELDWEED, DUNGWEED, WILD SPINACH, LAMBS QUARTERS, PIGWEED, MUCKWEED, DIRTY JOHN, ALL GOOD, DIRTY DICK
Season: March–October

The 'fat' in Fat Hen acknowledges the greasy nature of this herb's seeds, which were ground by the Anglo-Saxons into flour. Abundant in early England, it gave its name 'melde' to settlements such as Melbourn in Cambridgeshire. More recently it was gathered as a green vegetable, until usurped by its close but cultivated kin, spinach. This is a pity: few weeds are more packed with iron, calcium, protein, vitamins B_1 and B_2. Tollund Man, who knew a thing or two about hunter-gathering, included Fat Hen in his last meal, around 400 BC, before being preserved in his Danish peat bog.

Where to find Fat Hen? The clue is in those local names which trail the perfume of farmyard. It likes nitrogen-rich soil, such as muck heaps and well fertilised pastureland. The plant grows spire-shaped up to 1m tall, with reddish stems, grey-green oval leaves, usually covered when young in a white, powdery meal ('album' in the plant's scientific name refers to this white dust). The seeds are almost 2mm in diameter and frequently have a criss-cross pattern.

The young leaves and shoots can be cooked like spinach. They are delicious plunge-boiled then drained and mixed with butter, lemon juice, grated Parmesan, and salt and pepper. Alternatively, they can be chopped into stews, or be the mainstay of soup.

If you fancy making Fat Hen flour be warned: the labour needed is fabulous. Wait until July or August when the seeds are rusty pink, and strip into a basket. Spread on a tarpaulin or a sheet in the sun, turning occasionally. This might take two days or more, so bring in at night. Then rub, winnow and grind. The taste is reminiscent of buckwheat.

FAT HEN QUICHE

Serves 4

220g shortcut pastry
650g Fat Hen
1 onion, chopped
30g butter
10 tbsp milk
2 eggs
2 tbsp single cream
150g Parmesan, finely grated
pepper to taste

Unless you can make pastry, or charm someone into making pastry, buy it. Roll out the however acquired pastry. Rub some margarine around a 15cm flan ring and line with the pastry. Put into the fridge to cool.

Wash the Fat Hen, discard any thick stalks, and boil in salted water for 5 minutes. Strain and drain. When cool, chop finely.

Preheat the oven to 200°C/Gas Mark 6. Line the pastry case with greaseproof paper, fill with dried lentils (or anything small and relatively heavy); this is to prevent the pastry bubbling during cooking. Place in the oven and cook for 15 minutes; take out the flan, remove the weights, and cook for another 10 minutes. This is known as 'baking blind'.

Take out the flan case, and turn down the oven to 150°C/Gas Mark 2. Cook the onion gently in butter until golden.

Mix the milk, eggs and cream together in a large bowl with a fork. Add the Fat Hen, onion and Parmesan, and season with pepper. Since the Parmesan is salty you should not need extra sodium chloride. Pour the mixture into the flan case. Bake in the centre of the oven for 30 minutes. Check that the filling has 'set'. If it is still runny, cook for another 5 minutes.

FAT HEN PASTA SAUCE

1 red onion, peeled
2 cloves garlic, peeled and chopped
2 tbsp extra virgin olive oil
200g Fat Hen
1 ripe avocado, flesh scooped out
1 cup pine nuts
30g Kalamata olives
1 tbsp shoyu
100g Watercress
½ tsp paprika
2 tbsp water

Sweat the onion and garlic in the olive oil. Pour into a food processor, and add all the remaining ingredients and whizz. If too thick add a little water.

GIANT PUFFBALL   *Calvatia gigantea*
Season: June–September

Giant Puffballs live up to their name, sometimes growing bigger than a regulation FA football. The largest recorded specimen reached 120cm across, although the usual size of the fruit body is 5–80cm. Only pick specimens, however, that are young, white, firm, with a surface like kid-leather. They should sound hollow when tapped. Discard any that, when cut open, are yellow inside because they have passed their prime.

The Giant Puffball grows in pastureland, gardens, parks, woodland edges and hedgerows, and usually in the same spot year upon year, and mostly in fairy rings. It comes up after rain.

There is no adequate way of preserving *Calvatia gigantea* except to cook it in mushroom dishes and freeze them. It is extremely versatile in the kitchen, with a discernible earthy taste and meaty texture. Wipe over with a slightly damp cloth, slice, and add to casseroles, soups, and stews. You will not go far wrong if you fry it in slices for breakfast, either as accompaniment to bacon and eggs, or on top of brown toast. Dip the slices into a bowl of seasoned flour, shake off any excess, then dunk in beaten egg. Fry in hot extra virgin olive oil for 1–2 minutes, then turn over and repeat. Lift out with a slotted spatula.

In past times, the Giant Puffball was gathered and dried as fuel for the fire. According to the venerable Gerard, the dried mushroom was also used by beekeepers 'to kill or smother their Bees when they would drive the Hives and bereave the poore Bees of their meate, house and combs'.

Some smaller edible Puffballs to look out for are the Meadow Puffball (*Vascellum pratense*), the Mosaic Puffball (*Calvatia utriformis*), and Common Puffball (*Lycoperdon perlatum*), the latter mostly found in woodlands.

GOOD KING HENRY
Chenopodium bonus-henricus
Local Names: ALL GOOD, WILD SPINACH, MERCURY, SHOEMAKER'S HEELS, MIDDEN MYLIES, GOOSEFOOT, LINCOLNSHIRE SPINACH
Season: April–June

The Tudor herbalist Gerard observed that Good King Henry grew in 'untilled fields, and among rubbish near common ways, old walls, and by hedges in fields'. Being a liker of nitrogen and moisture this pot-herb, a member of the Goosefoot family, is still to be found in such places, as well as farmyards, which explains the local name 'Midden Mylies'.

The young springtime shoots can be prepared in the manner of asparagus, while the leaves can be chopped, then boiled or steamed like spinach. They do not make good salad because they go limp almost immediately on picking. A good source of iron and vitamin C, Good King Henry's leaves also contain high amounts of oxalic acid; these give the leaves their slightly sharp, acidic 'bite', but also mean that the plant needs to be eaten in moderation. As the summer progresses leaves accumulate saponins, making them unpalatably bitter.

Good King Henry is a tall erect perennial (up to 60cm), with its small greenish flowers borne on a terminal spike; the leaves are triangular, about 5cm in length, with wavy margins and a powdery surface.

LADY'S SMOCK   *Cardamine pratensis*
Local Names: MILKMAIDS, CUCKOOFLOWER, CUCKOO'S SHOES AND STOCKINGS, LADY'S MANTLE, LADY'S GLOVE, LACY'S SMOCK, MEADOW BITTERCRESS
Season: April–May

Is abundant in damp meadows, where its pale pink flowers bloom to meet the arrival of the cuckoo in April. Do not uproot, but pick young leaves, which are peppery, for salads and sandwich fillings. Alternatively chop leaves finely to make a green sauce for fish, or use in place of **Watercress** in soup. In eras gone by, this mineral and vitamin-packed plant was found on market stalls. It gets its Latin name *Cardamine pratensis* from two Greek sources, one meaning 'Watercress', alluding to its flavour, the other from its medicinal value as a heart drug.

A perennial in the wallflower family, reaching 60cm tall on an erect stem, with a defined basal rosette, Lady's Smock is found the kingdom over. The plants you leave behind will act as the food for orange-tip butterflies. Witches allegedly used Lady's Smocks in their spells; this was one reason why the flowers were never brought into the home.

PARASOL MUSHROOM
Macrolepiota procera
Season: July–October

Growing up to 30cm in height, the Parasol looms above the grass in fields cropped by sheep and cattle, though you will find it also in glades and rides in woodlands. The cap is initially bell-shaped, before opening into a scaly-brown canopy of 20cm or more. Adding to the impression of a parasol is, in the mature specimen, a movable ring on the grey snakeskin stem; this truly does look like the sliding runner by which a parasol is raised and lowered. The base of the snake-skin stem is bulbous. The scent is mealy.

Mature caps should be peeled, otherwise slice and go. This excellent mushroom will retain flavour and texture whether pan fried (with butter and pepper, plus a quick burst of lemon juice on serving), grilled, souped, stewed, or casseroled. Drying is the best means of preservation.

The Shaggy Parasol Mushroom (*Macrolepiota rhacodes* or *Chlorophyllum rhacodes*) differs from the above species in being half the size, with buff scales on the cap, and white flesh that reddens when bruised or cut. Frequently listed as edible, the Shaggy should be approached with caution; there are reports of people suffering an allergic reaction on first consumption. Always cook first, and only try a small amount.

Both the Parasol and Shaggy Parasol can be confused with the False Parasol. The latter has green spores; the former two Parasols have white spores.

PIGNUT   *Conopodium majus*
Local Names: EARTHNUT, DEVIL'S BREAD, ARNUT, CUCKOO POTATO, FAIRY POTATO, HOGNUT, JACKY-JOURNALS
Season: May–July

In *The Tempest*, Caliban digs up Pignuts with his fingers. You'll need a trowel – even a gardening spade – to root out this tuber treasure from 15cm under the earth.

The Pignut is a member of the carrot family, and has the delicate ferny leaves distinctive of the genus. The white swaying flower, which appears in May–June gawking over the grass, is the clue and cue needed to forage the tuber. Follow the thin stem down to earth, hold, and dig up the clod around it; with the utmost care break the clod around the point the stem enters the soil, and follow the immensely fragile single root down to the tuber. This is round, often with a black skin, and varies in size from Hazelnut to Walnut. Replace the clod.

Pignuts can be eaten on the spot, by simply scraping off the earth and outer husk with a thumb nail. But it may be wiser to wash them before consumption. Their taste is somewhere between coconut and parsnip. They are good in a vegetarian cutlet, but patience is needed to gather enough for a feast. Even in a Pignut hotspot, I can usually gather no more than one every 5 minutes.

The plant is widespread throughout the isles, common in field edges, shady banks and woods. Don't forget that current legislation requires the landowner's approval before the digging up of Pignuts.

One warning. The Pignut was once commonly believed to be an aphrodisiac.

POPPY *Papaver rhoeas*
Local Names: CORN POPPY, FIELD POPPY, CORN ROSE, CHEESEBOWLS, COCK'S HEAD, POPPET, RED CAP
Season: July–September

The Poppy likes disturbed ground, which explains why it flourished in the shell-torn earth of the Western Front in the First World War. An erect annual, with the famous blood-red flower, its autumn seeds are edible – and not in the least narcotic, unlike those of the opium variant. To gather the seeds, cut off the ripe, dry 'pepper-pot' heads in early autumn and shake in a paper bag to release the blue-black specks. These are widely used in baking as decoration, but also as flavouring. An oil extracted from the seeds finds its way onto the artist's palette, as well as the kitchen shelf.

Be aware that, with the exception of the seeds, all parts of the Poppy are mildly toxic.

SAINT GEORGE'S MUSHROOM
Calocybe gambosa
Season: April–June

One of the earliest mushrooms of the year, making it difficult to confuse with any other. Traditionally, *Calocybe gambosa* appears on 23 April, the day commemorating England's patron saint, although with global warming it seems to make its bow earlier and earlier in the month.

The cap is between 3–15cm across and is white; the gills and stem are likewise white, with the mushroom no more than 7cm tall. To be found in unimproved pastureland and parks, hedges and mixed woodland, often growing in 'fairy rings', some of which may be hundreds of years old. When picking, always cut the stem with a knife to avoid damaging the mycelia rings. The mushroom has a distinct mealy odour and taste. Sauté in olive oil with crushed garlic, seasoning with chopped parsley, salt and pepper. Serve on brown bread toast. It also goes well with chicken in a casserole.

The solid flesh of the St George's Mushroom makes it ideal for pickling. In a saucepan boil up white wine vinegar and water in a ratio of 2:1, then add the mushrooms and a tablespoon of salt, and cook for 15 minutes. Extract the mushrooms with a slotted spoon, and leave to cool on a dry cloth (a tea towel is ideal). Transfer the mushrooms to a sterilised preserving jar, push them down tightly and cover with olive oil. To avoid the danger of botulism, it is imperative that the oil covers the mushroom completely, and reaches to the top of the jar. Close the lid tightly. With this done, the mushrooms should last a year. If you choose, you can add dried herbs for taste and decoration before sealing.

SALAD BURNET　*Sanguisorba minor*
Local Names: DRUM STICKS, OLD MAN'S PEPPER, BURNET, RED KNOBS
Season: February–October

Common on chalk downs and dry grassland in the south, Salad Burnet – no surprise, given its name – is a traditional ingredient in green salads, and was once extensively cultivated for the plate before falling out of fashion. The dainty young leaves, which can be picked from spring to early autumn, have the taste and smell of cucumber. Introduce the leaves into garnishes, herb butters, herb dips, soft cheese, casseroles and soups. The leaves can be dried and in this state make, with a pinch of **Rosemary** and **Thyme**, a useful flavouring for baked or grilled fish. Coarse leaves can be steamed as a green vegetable.

Like **Borage**, Salad Burnet was, in times past, used in the brewing industry to 'cool' and flavour ale, while Gerard considered that leaves put in wine 'yeeldeth a certain grace in the drinking'. If a liquid use for Salad Burnet is your desire, try a few bruised leaves in your summer Pimms, punch or lemonade. The World War II forager Jason Hill recommended 'Burnet Vinegar' made so:

Fill a stone or glass jar loosely with the leaves, fill up with vinegar, stand it in a cool place for a week and then pour the vinegar on to another lot of leaves; at the end of another week strain and bottle.

Somewhat further back in time, Francis Bacon suggested that Salad Burnet be set in garden walkways alongside **Wild Thyme** and Mint, 'to perfume the air most delightfully, being trodden on and crushed'. As well as delighting the nose, the upright herb is good on the eye, with a rosette of graceful stems supporting toothed leaves. The flower heads, which appear in late spring and early summer on stems up to 40cm tall, are tight balls packed with greenish-white flowers with a reddish tinge.

WILD HERB DIP
150ml carton sour cream or Quark
8 chopped stalks (with leaves) Salad Burnet
2 chopped shoots Mint
6 chopped chives
salt and pepper

Add the herbs and seasoning to the sour cream, and stir in with a fork. Serve with cucumber and carrot sticks, vegetable or potato chips.

SHEPHERD'S PURSE
Capsella bursa-pastoris
Local Names: MONEY BAGS, NAUGHTY MAN'S PLAYTHING, BAD MAN'S OATMEAL, PEPPER AND SALT, LADY'S PURSE, PICK POCKET, GENTRY'S PURSE
Season: Throughout the year

'The Naughty Man' and 'Bad Man' in the folk names for *Capsella bursa-pastoris* is, of course, the Devil. There is, however, nothing evil about this small annual (sometimes biennial) plant . . . except for its tendency, if you are a farmer or gardener, to rapidly multiply and take over your land.

Kinder are the names which refer to its 6–9mm seed capsule, which does indeed look like a medieval purse, bag or case (capsella) when inverted. Break open the ripe purse, and the seeds fall out, like coins. 'Money Bags', indeed.

Medicinally, Shepherd's Purse leaves were used as an anti-scorbutic, anti-diuretic and Gervase Markham's *The English Hus-Wife*, 1615, advised it in a preparation for dysentery or diarrhoea:

To cure the worst bloody flux that may be, take a quart of red wine, and a spoonful of cumin seed, boyle them together until half be consumed, then take knot-grass, and Shepherde-purse, and Plantane, and stamp them severall, and then strain them, and take of the juice of each . . . a good spoonful; and put them to the wine, and so seeth them again a little; then drink it lukewarm, half over night and half the next morning.

Modern herbalists advise the herb's use to stem internal and external bleeding, except in pregnant women since it can cause uterine contractions.

Oddly, Shepherd's Purse does not seem to have been eaten much in days gone by. Or at least none of its country names suggest it being put on the platter. However, all the green parts are edible, and have a slight 'bite' without being bitter. They provide vitamins C, A, K and the minerals sulphur, iron, potassium, sodium, plus the neurotransmitter acetycholine. When young, Shepherd's Purse has something of the Dandelion about it, beginning as a basal rosette of toothed leaves. In mid spring the plant takes an upward leap, with erect flower stalks that can reach 60cm; the flowers are white, four-petaled and form a cross.

Use the leaves in salads, coleslaw and stir-fries. They are best picked before the flowers emerge in April.

SILVERWEED *Potentilla anserina*

Local Names: TRAVELLER'S EASE, GOLDEN SOVEREIGNS, BREAD AND BUTTER, TANSY, GOLDEN FLOWER, MOSS-CORNS, SILVER FEATHER

Season: September–November

In times of famine in the Middle Ages, the roots of Silverweed were 'roasted, boiled or ground down into a kind of floure'. Silverweed was even cultivated in the harsh Highlands and Islands of Scotland, where it was claimed that 'A man could sustain himself on Silverweed from a square of ground'. The taste is slightly and pleasantly reminiscent of parsnip, but a fearsome amount of toil required to dig-up a meal's worth of the insubstantial roots. Take a spade or digging stick. Mature plants growing in soft, well-drained soil provide the biggest, most rewarding tubers. Wash well, and scrape off the dark outer skin with a potato-peeler. The tissue underneath is brilliant white, starchy, and highly digestible.

Above ground, Silverweed is conspicuously beautiful, with feather-like silvery leaves perfectly framing the bright yellow flower. In height, it reaches 20cm. You'll find it on roadsides all round Britain, plus dunes and waste ground.

Use the roots as you would parsnips. Historically, the leaves were used for wine, or for putting in the shoes of travellers to reduce swellings ('Traveller's Ease'). Herbalists advised the use of root and leaf extracts in the curing of toothache, wounds to the genitalia, and stomach upsets.

Early autumn is the best time to harvest the roots, when the leaves turn orange.

SORREL   *Rumex acetosa*

Local Names: LONDON GREEN SAUCE, SOLDIERS, SOUR GRASS, BREAD AND CHEESE.

Season: Throughout the year, but especially March–September

The clue to Sorrel's usefulness in the wild food pantry is in the name: Sorrel is a corruption of the Old French *surele*, meaning sour. This quality Sorrel surely has, but in a nicely sharp, lemony manner. Until the time of Henry VIII Sorrel was cultivated as a herb and used principally in a 'Green Sauce' for fish. Sorrel's Latin name means roughly 'suck vinegar', because agricultural workers chewed the leaves to slake their thirst. Try biting or sucking a leaf yourself: your mouth will flood with saliva.

The dark spear-like leaves of Sorrel (rumex being a type of Roman javelin) are reminiscent of **Docks**, of which genus it is a member. The plant is plentiful in pastureland untreated by chemicals, especially liking acid clays, and tends to grows in thick clumps. In summer, the spires of red flowers of Sorrel impart a red mist to meadows waiting to be cut for hay. Sorrel is quite remarkably hardy, and can be found even in winter. The young leaves are the tenderest and tastiest, and can simply be washed and added to a salad, or shredded into cream cheese for a bread spread. I like to put them in with new potatoes, olive oil and seasoning. Older leaves may need the veins cut out, and should be cooked like spinach. And like spinach it vanishes during cooking. Put in lots. And always use stainless steel utensils for Sorrel, because iron or aluminium reacts with the high oxalic acid content (the chemical that gives the plant its 'bite') and affects the taste.

Sorrel makes the easiest sauce known to man or woman: the Tudor 'Green Sauce' was ground Sorrel leaves with sugar and vinegar added. A modern take is to shred 200g of Sorrel leaves, gently melt a knob of butter in a pan, add the shredded Sorrel leaves and stir until wilted. Then stir in a heaped tablespoon of crème fraiche. Postle for one minute. Serve.

Sorrel has a special liking for eggs. Try chopped, washed Sorrel leaves folded into an omelette.

SORREL SOUP

Serves 4

It is always tempting to add cream to soups; do not add cream to Sorrel soup because it will curdle. This makes Sorrel soup ideal for the lactose intolerant.

30 Sorrel leaves
1 medium potato
1 medium onion
25g butter
1.2 litres chicken stock
sea salt and black pepper

Wash the Sorrel leaves, and if necessary strip out the spine. Slice the potato and chop the onion. Melt the butter in a saucepan, and fry the onion until it softens. Add the potato and continue cooking for a few minutes. Tip in the Sorrel leaves, and cook until the Sorrel wilts. Pour in the chicken stock, and cook on a low heat until the potato is soft. Transfer to a blender and process. Season and serve immediately.

YARROW   *Achillea millefolium*

Local Names: NOSEBLEED PLANT, THOUSAND-LEAF, SNEEZEWORT, WOUND WORT, STANCH-GRISS, YARRA
Season: March–October

There is probably more folklore attached to Yarrow than any other weed. For the Ancient Greeks, Yarrow was the plant Achilles used to bind the wounds of his soldiers at Troy (hence the first part of its Latin name); for the Chinese the counting of dried Yarrow stalks was held to be indispensable in divining the *I Ching*, the Book of Changes; the Celts were convinced the herb had psychotropic tendencies that allowed the imbiber to see their future spouse.

All this, and it makes very nice tea too.

Common in pastureland and wasteland, Yarrow is a perennial with long multi-divided green leaves (thus 'millefolium',

'Thousand-Leaf') which would pass for feather boas for little people. Flowers are creamy white discs at the end of the stems, which can reach 60cm in height. Yarrow can be found almost the year round, but mainly occurs between May and October.

To make tea, take 3 leaves and infuse in a cup of boiling water for 4–5 minutes. Strain and serve. Sweeten with honey if required.

The tea can be made equally well with dried Yarrow leaves.

Very long leaves can be served in salads or steamed as green vegetables, but the amaroidal taste is to the liking of few. Set against pasta, though, it looks magnificent. In the past, the bitterness of Yarrow lent itself to the brewing industry which used it to flavour ale. Modern imbibers of vodka sometimes flavour the spirit with Yarrow heads.

A caveat: extended use of Yarrow can cause sensitivity of the skin and eyes. And enable you to see fairies. If you put it up your nose it will allow you to know if your love is reciprocated. At the cost of a tell-tale nosebleed:

Yarroway, Yarroway, bear a white blow
If my love love me, my nose will bleed now

7

THE WOOD

ASH *Fraxinus excelsior*
Local Name: WHINSHAG
Season: July–August

The fruits of the Ash are commonly called 'keys' because they hang in bunches reminiscent of the keys of a medieval gaoler. Singly the fruit looks like the wing of a locust, with the edible part, which is the size of a pine nut, located at the stem end. Ash keys are widely and wildly rumoured to be pleasant eating when first ripe and de-skinned. I have never found them to be anything but screw-face astringent: raw, they taste of wormwood. And pickled they taste of wormwood. Those who love them say they taste like capers and are a piquant addition to cold cuts of meat and oily fish.

If you wish to pickle Ash keys, pick fruits which are still green. And never shelter under the tree when a storm breaks because according to the old country saw

Avoid an Ash
It courts the flash

On the other hand, if confronted with an adder, you may wish to seek refuge under the Ash, since according to the selfsame ancient folklore adders so loathed *Fraxinus excelsior* that they would rather flee through fire than through its leaves.

Common throughout Britain in woodland, but also in hedgerows, the Ash reaches 25m, its grey bark at first smooth but acquiring vertical fissures as it ages. Buds are black, and the leaves appear as 3–6 pairs of lateral leaflets. Leafy branches used to be given to livestock as fodder, and the wood, which is readily bent, was valued in the making of oars, ploughs, fork handles and hockey sticks. Ash wood, as John Evelyn remarked, is 'the sweetest of our forest fuelling, and the fittest for the Ladies chamber', and will even burn when it is green. Somewhat handily, the burning of Ash wood is said to banish the Devil. The seed keys appear only on female trees.

PICKLED ASH KEYS

Recipes for pickled Ash keys are many and ancient. This one is loosely based on that of Jason Hill in *Wild Foods of Great Britain*, 1939. In some parts of the country, the keys are known as 'kitty-keys'.

Pick tender green keys and boil in two changes of water to remove the bitterness. Strain. Heat up a mixture of 250ml vinegar and 250ml cider. Pour over the keys, then add a dash of salt, a couple of cloves, pinch of peppercorns and table-spoon of Demerara sugar. Put in a heatproof dish in a warm oven for one hour to infuse. Allow to cool before sealing in pickling jars.

Infused in hot water, the keys also make a herbal drink reputedly beneficial in the treatment of skin conditions and leprosy.

BEECH TREE *Fagus sylvatica*
Season: October–November

The fruits of the Beech, known as nuts or mast, are sharply triangular and are exquisitely packed in a bristly green husk, and are only ripe when this outer casing splits. Beech mast has long been appreciated as a foodstuff by mankind, and even longer by a whole host of animals, including squirrels, wild boar, deer, jays, badgers and mice.

Beech trees do not crop every year, but every three or four years, when the harvest is likely to be heavy. Collect as soon as possible in autumn, before the nuts are all taken by the animal and bird competition, and store in single layers in a ventilated cardboard box (make holes by twisting a knife) in a warm room.

Some 20 per cent of the Beech nut is comprised of a thick, sweetish yellow oil that is excellent for frying. To extract the oil pulverise the nuts in an electric grinder, or have a Jane Fonda work-out by pulverising them in a mortar with a pestle, and squeeze the resultant pulp through a sieve/muslin bag, or failing this a pair of washed stockings. A kilo and half of mast should give you about 250g of oil. The oil is best if you can be bothered to de-shell each nut, and even better if you scrape off the slightly astringent skin of the kernel. But this is a fiddly operation.

Beech oil was commercially produced in Britain until the middle of the Victorian era, and is still preferred in some French cooking circles over the ubiquitous olive oil.

Beech mast is mildly toxic raw, so cook before eating. That said, it can be used neat to flavour gin. *Fagus* is derived from the Greek *Phegos*, meaning 'edible, for eating', and this elegant tall tree (which can reach over 40m) also provides springtime lime-green leaves that may be popped into salads or soups. In World War II, Hitler's regime tried drying the leaves as a substitute for tobacco in cigarettes.

The tree is native to southern England, and introduced elsewhere. It is rare in Scotland.

ROASTED BEECH NUTS

Remove the kernels, place on a baking sheet and sprinkle with extra virgin olive oil. Bake at 180°C/Gas Mark 4 until golden. Drain on kitchen towel, toss in ground sea salt, and eat as a party nibble.

BEEFSTEAK FUNGUS *Fistulina hepatica*

Local Names: BLEEDING-BRACKET TOADSTOOL, OAK-TONGUE, OX-TONGUE

Season: August–November

Beefsteak fungus looks uncommonly like a liver protruding from a tree trunk, which is reflected in the second part of its Latin name. When cut, the flesh oozes blood-red juice. It is reassuringly difficult to confuse with anything else.

Nearly all broad-leaved trees will host the Beefsteak, though its preference is for **Oak** and **Sweet Chestnut**, and it tends to appear year after year on the same tree. The brackets of the fungus can reach 25cm across. They can also be dispiritingly high off the ground; I have come across them 10m up on Oaks. Widespread, but sometimes difficult to harvest, throughout Britain.

In taste, Beefsteak is as acidic as it is meaty. The sourness can be neutralized by cutting the Beefsteak into strips and soaking overnight in milk. Try grilling like the steak from which it takes its name. Young specimens can be eaten raw.

HERB-CRUSTED BEEFSTEAK

Serves 4

600g sliced Beefsteak mushroom
500ml white wine
2 tbsp chopped parsley
50g plain flour
salt and pepper
1 large egg, beaten
150g breadcrumbs
1 tbsp *fines herbes*
1 tbsp extra virgin olive oil

Marinade the sliced Beefsteak in the wine and parsley for 30 minutes.

To make the herb crust, spread the flour on a plate and season with salt and pepper. Place the beaten egg in a bowl, and stir in the breadcrumbs and herbs.

Shake the mushrooms dry in a clean tea towel, and dip into the flour, brushing off any excess, then dip into the eggy breadcrumbs. Fry in the olive oil, 1–2 minutes each side. Drain on kitchen paper. Serve with salad and a full-bodied red wine.

CEP *Boletus edulis*
Local Names: PENNY BUN, KING BOLETTE, STICKY BUN
Season: August–November

The Cep is the selfsame Porcini that people jostle for in the deli aisle at Waitrose. Usually 8–20cm or so in diameter, the cap of the Cep is convex but becomes flatter as the mushroom matures; cap colour ranges from light to tawny with a distinctive sticky sheen in damp weather that exactly explains its popular name of 'Penny Bun', since it is then the visual twin of a sugar-glazed sticky bun. Under the cap, there are creamy-coloured pores instead of gills. The stem is bulbous, paler than the cap, with a network of fine white 'veins'. *Boletus edulis* is found in coniferous and deciduous woodland, especially in **Beech** woods, sometimes singly, sometimes in groups. Keep your eyes peeled particularly in glades.

When you gather the mushroom, cut off with a knife. Wipe off any dirt and do not wash or peel. The Cep has a wonderful nutty flavour and the firm white flesh allows versatility in cooking. The mushroom and its broth can be used in soups, stews, sautés, stir-fries; it can be sliced raw into salads, and whole caps can be grilled, fried, or baked. The mushroom is also good enough to be the feature in its dishes, such as Porcini Pasta, or Porcini Risotto. Low in fat, the Cep is high in protein, vitamins and minerals.

Drying is the best method of preservation, and you can dry the mushroom whole or in slices.

The Cep is one of the easiest mushrooms to identify, but do not be blasé about identification; in 2008 Nicholas Evans, author of *The Horse Whisperer*, mistook Deadly Webcap

(*Cortinarius speciosissimus*) for Cep and poisoned his family, who subsequently required dialysis and renal transplants.

Porcini, incidentally, means 'pig food'. But these delicious mushrooms are wasted on swine.

A quick and failsafe method of cooking Ceps to perfection is to pre-heat the oven to 200°C/Gas Mark 6, and put the Ceps into a large square of baking foil along with crushed garlic, bay leaves, sprigs of **Rosemary** and **Wild Thyme**, and a shake of black pepper. Fold the foil to make a loose parcel and stand in a baking tray containing 1cm of water (this prevents the mushrooms burning underneath) in the oven for 25 minutes or so.

MUSHROOM RISOTTO

Serves 4

This risotto works well with any wild mushrooms, as long as the mix includes something flavourful, such as Ceps or Morels.

200g mixed wild mushrooms
1.5 litres chicken or vegetable stock
3 tbsp extra virgin olive oil
2 shallots, finely chopped
2 cloves garlic
salt and pepper
1 sprig Rosemary, stripped
200g Arborio or other risotto rice
10g dried Ceps, reconstituted by adding boiling water
large glass dry white wine
freshly grated Parmesan
25g butter
25g flat leaf parsley, finely chopped

Wash the fresh mushrooms, and cut into strips if large. Put the stock in a saucepan and bring up to a simmer.

Heat the oil in a heavy bottomed saucepan and fry the shallots until soft. Crush the garlic with a big pinch of salt to make a paste. Stir into the shallots together with the

Rosemary leaflets. Add the rice to the pan and coat each grain in olive oil. Then add the wild mushrooms, stir fry for 2–3 minutes, before adding the reconstituted Ceps in their soaking water. Then gently ladle in the warm stock, stirring all the while. Let each ladleful be absorbed before adding the next. The amount of stock is approximate; you need just enough to cook the rice.

When the rice is nearly *al dente*, after about 15–20 minutes, add the wine, and stir until the liquid is absorbed.

Remove from the pan. Add the grated Parmesan, butter and pepper. Serve immediately, with a sprinkling of the parsley on top of each serving.

CHANTERELLE *Cantharellus cibarius*
Local Name: GIROLLE
Season: June–November

The Chanterelle is an object of beauty. Egg-yolk yellow in colour, its mature cap is a graceful, fluted and flared bowl. The Latin name for the genus comes from *cantharus*, 'a drinking goblet'. The pedestal or stem, extends to 6cm in height, tapers towards the base, and is the same colour as the cap. Chanterelles often grow in colonies, making the illusion of a cloth of gold dropped onto the ground.

Less poetically, if you want to know what a Chanterelle looks like, head to an upmarket supermarket: the mushroom has become an indispensable adjunct to home gastronomics.

In the wild, the mushroom is to be found over most of the UK in summer and autumn. A lover of acid soils, it often nestles below Birch, **Beech** and **Oak** in woods, though I have found it in open grassland. To harvest, cut off at ground level with a sharp knife. Insects also find Chanterelles to their liking, so take care not to take a zoo home with you. The Chanterelle will dry reasonably well (string on a cord in a dry, warm place), though some of the pleasing and distinctive apricot odour is lost. Use in stews and soups, omelettes and pasta dishes, or mix with scrambled eggs.

This esculent fungus can be confused with the False Chanterelle, a denizen of coniferous woods. However, the False Chanterelle is bereft of the distinctive apricot odour.

STEWED CHANTERELLES ON TOAST

Serves 4

I have hidden the bad news. Chanterelles can be tough. This recipe works even on the biggest and baddest.

55g butter
1 clove garlic
250g Chanterelles, sliced
2 tbsp white wine
salt and pepper

Melt a knob of butter in a frying pan on a low heat, add the garlic and Chanterelles and sauté. Then pour in the wine and add a pinch of salt. Cover and cook on low heat for about 20 minutes. Serve on toasted and buttered granary bread.

CRAB APPLE   *Malus sylvestris*

Local Names: SOUR GRABS, SCARB, BITTERSGALL, GRIBBLE, SCROGG
Season: October–November

Malus sylvestris is native to Europe, and is the ancestor of the cultivated apple. You'll find it growing in woodland or near abandoned settlements, forming a small deciduous tree of up to 10m in height, which bears white, pink-tinged flowers in May. The fruit, which ripens in October, is almost globular, and is a sickly yellow-green in colour, blushed with red if reached by the sun. A Crab tree in full fruit, almost bursting with little apples, is an uplifting sight to counter the greyest day.

The true wild Crab differs from cultivated and feral apples ('wildings') in being thorny, the smallness of its fruit (2cm or so) and having hairless leaves and flower stalks. Very few true

Crabs exist; you are much more likely to encounter a wilding
Crab that has grown from the pip in a discarded core. This is
especially true if the Crab tree before you is growing in a
hedge or by the roadside.

The country names for Crabs serve as a warning to the
unwary biter of this wild fruit: it is mouth-puckeringly acid.
The astringent fruit gave rise to the English word 'crabby',
meaning bad-tempered. In medieval times, Crab Apples were
the source of the sour sauce *verjuice*, that era's equivalent of
the modern cook's lemon.

You will need to sweeten your Crabs in the cooking.

Crab Apple jelly is the best known way to use the fruits, not
least because they are pectin rich and help setting. But there is
another very worthwhile use to which Crab Apples can be put;
when Caesar invaded Britain in 55 BC he found the Celtic
natives fermenting the juice of *Malus sylvestris*. The Romans
titled the drink 'Sicera'. Cider.

CRAB APPLE JELLY

Makes 2–4kg

Ideal on toast for breakfast, or as an accompaniment to roast
meat.

4kg Crab Apples
1 lemon
2kg caster sugar

Wash and quarter the Crab Apples, but leave in the cores
because they contain heaps of the pectin necessary to set the
jelly. Put the apples in a large heavy pan or cauldron with just
enough water to cover them. Bring to the boil and simmer
until the fruit is pulpy and soft (about 25–30 minutes).

You now need to pour the pulp into a jelly bag (or double
layers of muslin) and let drip into a pan overnight. Tying the
corners of the bag to an upside down stool with a bowl underneath to catch the apple drips is the ideal arrangement. If you
hurry the process by squeezing the bag this will make the jelly

cloudy; if you are unworried by aesthetics, squeeze every last drop out.

Next morning, measure the apple juice and add sugar at the ratio of 500g sugar to 1 litre juice. Tip into a saucepan, add the juice of the lemon and bring to the boil, stirring with a wooden spoon to dissolve the sugar. Remove any surface scum. Boil hard for 10 minutes, then test for setting point with a sugar thermometer: this is 105°C. Alternatively, have a fridge-chilled pudding-spoon on standby: put a small amount of the jelly on the back of the spoon. If it solidifies it is set. If it is still liquid, boil some more, then repeat the test.

When setting point is reached, remove from the heat and ladle the jelly into warm sterilised jars. Cover with a waxed paper disc, tightly seal with a lid, and store in a cool dark place. The jelly should keep for a year. A more savoury jelly can be obtained by adding herbs, such as Sage and **Rosemary**.

The above recipe for Crab Apple jelly can be used as the model for a 'Hedgerow Jelly' using Rosehips, Hawthorn haws, Blackthorn sloes, Bullaces, Rowanberries, Elderberries, and Blackberries in any proportions you can forage, as long as the mix includes 50 per cent of the high pectin Crab Apple.

ELDER   *Sambucus nigra*
Local Names: JUDAS TREE, DEVIL'S WOOD, GOD'S STINKING TREE, BLACK ELDER, BOUR, SCAW, DOG TREE
Season: June (flowers), September–October (berries)

With its fissured trunk and tendency to loll, the Elder tree is not a thing of natural beauty. Yet from such arboreal ugliness emerges in early summer a large (20cm across) white flower that is a glory to eye and nose.

And tongue. Snip off the fragrant, nectar-rich clusters of Elderflower and shake to remove unwanted insectoid protein. The heads make an instant snack in their raw state, and a quick one frittered. Hold the baubles of blossom by the stem, dip into a batter of flour and egg, fry, and sprinkle with sugar.

Traditionally, of course, the flowers impart their muscatel flavour to that iconic drink of the British summer, Elderflower cordial. I prefer to turn the flowers into Elderflower champagne, for the simple reason that this drink captures in liquidity the oracular fizziness of the flower heads, which resemble showers of sparks.

By autumn the flower heads have turned into bright purple chandeliers of berries. Take only the lower bracts and leave the upper ones for the birds, especially migrating members of the thrush family, which adore them. The berries are replete with vitamin A (600 IU per 100mg), vitamin C (36mg per 100mg) and anti-oxidants. So, well worth the picking for a cordial-cum-tonic that will see you through a sniffling winter, and maybe more than that; John Evelyn thought that an extract of the berries was a 'catholicon against all infirmities whatever'. Elderberries can also be turned into a liqueur, and a rich, port-like wine. In historical times, the 'Englishman's grape' was grown commercially in Elder orchards.

Yet more things to do with the glut of Elderberries: they complement other fruits very well, and mixed with them will make beautiful pies and preserves. Such is the versatility of the berry, it can turn equally into a delicious ketchup, if simmered in equal parts cider and wine vinegar (just enough to cover the fruit in the saucepan), along with Thyme, Bay, **Fennel** and garlic salt. Bottle with a few peppercorms.

The tree, which can grow with almost the same haste as bamboo thrives pretty much everywhere, but relishes fertile soil, loaded with nitrogen and phosphorus. Aside from woodland, you'll find it by farmyards and rabbit warrens. Elderflower water is a well-known astringent, and is still listed in the British Pharmacopoeia as a lotion for eye and skin injuries.

The cruel country names for the Elder reflect the belief that it was an Elder from which Judas, Christ's betrayer, hanged himself. It is the Devil's own wood, and if burned in Warwickshire you'll see Lucifer himself coming down the chimney. For the same reason, the Irish have long forbade its use in the making of boats.

Almost worse, in merrie old Scotland, among other regions

of Britain, it was widely held that Christ himself was crucified on a cross made from Elder or 'Bour':

Bour-tree, bour-tree, crookit rung,
Never straight, and never strong,
Ever bush, and never tree
Since our Lord was nailed t'ye.

Doubtless some of the evil reputation of Elder is due to its nasty habit of killing Dark Age peasants as they lay shivering in their hovels. When burning, Elder wood releases cyanide.

ELDERBERRY CORDIAL
25 Elderberry heads
600ml water
225g honey

Place all the ingredients in a pan, bring to the boil, then simmer for 15 minutes, stirring occasionally. Leave loosely covered overnight before bottling, and consume within three months.

ELDERBERRY AND BLACKBERRY ICE CREAM
350g Elderberries
350g Blackberries
275ml double cream
40g icing sugar
2 egg whites

Cook the fruits together in a tablespoon or so of water. Liquidise, then sieve to separate out the pips. Whip the cream until it is thick enough to stand up, fold in the sugar and fruit purée. Whisk the egg whites until they are stiff, then fold them into the melange. Freeze in an old ice cream carton or similar plastic container.

ELDERFLOWER CHAMPAGNE

8 large Elderflower heads
4.5 litres cold water
¼ cup Wild Rose petals (if possible to obtain)
2 unwaxed lemons, sliced
2 tbsp cider vinegar
750g sugar
champagne yeast
collection of clean plastic drink bottles

Pick young florets, preferably in the morning when their aroma is at its strongest. Shake off the insects. The florets will not keep, so take them home as soon as you can, and in the kitchen 'fork off' (detach) any bits of stalk. This is bitter and will spoil your brew. If you can find them, **Wild Rose** petals add a subtle floral fragrance and pinkish hue.

Put the 4.5 litres of water into a large saucepan, together with the Elderflower heads, Wild Rose petals, the sliced lemon, and cider vinegar. Add the sugar and stir until dissolved. Sprinkle on the champagne yeast. Cover and leave to stand for twenty four hours, remembering to stir twice with a wooden spoon.

Using a jug, bale the liquid through a sieve into the plastic drinks bottles. Put the tops on loosely and place the bottles on a plastic tray out of direct sunlight. Over the next fortnight, the champagne will ferment. When it has almost stopped, screw down the caps and store in a cool place. Allow a day or two for the fizz to build up, then the champagne will be ready for drinking – but refrigerate before pouring. The champagne will keep for months, although becoming drier and more alcoholic as it ages.

Using plastic bottles means that you are more likely to avoid the calamity that sometimes strikes makers of Elderflower champagne: glass bottles exploding from the pressure of the fermentation process. To check the pressure on plastic bottles, simply give them a quick squeeze. If the bottle is turgid, gently unscrew the cap until the gas hisses out, then re-tighten.

HAZEL   *Corylus avellana*

Local Names: FILBERT, FILBEARD, COB, COBNUT, COBBLY-
CUT, NUTTALL, WOODNUT
Season: September–October

The Hazel is a shrubby tree found in woods and hedges,
distinctive for its grey bark, yellow catkins and nuts, the latter
encased in a hard shell which appears on the tree from August
to October. The English name derives from the Anglo-Saxon
haesel, meaning hat, in reference to the frilly cap in which the
nut sits.

The nomenclature might be medieval, but the culinary use
of Hazelnuts is prehistoric, and they formed an important item
in the diet of Mesolithic hunter-gatherers. Pick a Hazelnut to
eat and you are doing something that links you across time to
your very first forebears.

The nuts remain on the tree until ripe, falling off in early
autumn, by which time the cap and shell will have turned, or
be beginning to turn, brown. Before this the Hazelnut is
uselessly soft. In Normandy in the Middle Ages the tree was
allocated to Saint Philibert (Filbert) because this Benedictine
saint's day on 22 August was when the nuts were considered
ripe. Actually, 22 August is somewhat optimistic; try two
weeks later.

You'll find stiff local competition for the nuts, which are
avidly sought after by packs of animals and birds, led by the
squirrel and the jay.

The nuts can be stored in their shell in a cool, dry place for
weeks, even months, before use. They are extremely nutritious, containing proportionately more protein than a hen's
egg, as well as a significant amount of oil.

Using the nuts: in the raw state they can be chopped into
salads or onto yogurt, or ground up and added to biscuits and
cakes. I like to add the ground nuts to milk to make a
smoothie. Alternatively, 'Hazelnut milk' can be made by
soaking nuts overnight, draining, then whizzing in a blender at
the ratio of 1 part Hazelnuts to 3 parts water.

If anything, roasted Hazelnuts are an even more delicious treat. Put in the oven on a baking tray at 180°C/Gas Mark 4 for about 10 minutes, watching like a hawk to avoid burning. When cooled, rub off skins between your hands, and eat. Then again, the roast nuts can be crushed and added as topping to cakes and cereals. Or put in a jar and covered with honey, to be spooned out as a snack. They can even be pressed for a delicate oil ideal on salads or in cooking.

The Hazel, in folklore, is the Tree of Knowledge. Hazel sticks are the rods used for dowsing water.

HAZELNUT SHORTBREAD

300g shelled Hazelnuts
25g light brown sugar
300g butter
pinch ground allspice
110g rice flour
140g plain flour
icing sugar

Roast the Hazelnuts at 170°C/Gas Mark 3 for 5 minutes, remove, but leave the oven at this heat.

Put the Hazelnuts in a blender and whizz. Grease a large baking sheet.

Beat the sugar into the butter until soft, add the allspice, both flours and the blended nuts. Mix and sift until a thick, smooth paste is obtained.

Place a 15cm flan ring on the baking sheet and press the paste into shape. Remove the flan ring, and prick lightly with a fork.

Bake for 30 minutes in the oven. Leave to cool on a wire rack. Dust sparingly with icing sugar.

HAZELNUT AND MUSHROOM PÂTÉ

Serves 4

This makes a useful party nibble, a sandwich filling (with green salad), an *hors d'oeuve*.

1 small red onion, chopped
2 tbsp extra virgin olive oil
1 clove garlic, crushed
150g Porcini (Cep) or Chestnut mushrooms
1 tsp Cognac/brandy
100g roasted Hazelnuts
250g smoked tofu
1 tsp fresh Rosemary, chopped
1 tsp fresh Thyme, chopped
1 tsp shoyu
1 tbsp water
salt and freshly ground black pepper

Fry the onion in the olive oil until caramelised.

Add the garlic and mushrooms and fry over medium heat until the mushrooms soften. Remove well away from the heat and add the Cognac.

Put the Hazelnuts into a blender and blitz. Then add the tofu, herbs, shoyu and onion-mushroom mix from the pan and process until a firm paste emerges. You may need to add water. Season. Serve on toast.

HEN-OF-THE-WOODS   *Grifola frondosa*
Local Name: RAM'S HEAD
Season: September–November

Grows at the base of Oak and other deciduous trees throughout Britain in autumn, though is nowhere abundant. The fruit body consists of an uncontrolled mass of overlapping grey-brown fleshy fans (white underneath) which can reach 20kg in weight. No-one would accuse Hen-of-the-Woods of being a 10 in looks: the fungus' name is derived from its resemblance to the ruffled feathers of the back end of a chicken. On the other hand, few wild food seekers will fail to appreciate its firm texture, which lends the mushroom to stewing and casseroling, without losing its shape.

Do not pluck the whole fungus. Take only the youngest caps, those which do not bruise when touched, and rinse well before use. Dirt, grit and bits of bark become engrained in the caps, all of which may have to be pared away with a knife. As with other bracket fungi, Hen-of the-Woods appears annually in the same spot.

Hen-of-the-Woods can be preserved by drying, freezing or pickling. In health food shops it appears as 'Maitake' and is advertised as a means of beating cancer and boosting the immune system.

PAN-ROASTED HEN-OF-THE-WOODS

Serves 4

500g Hen-of-the-Woods
salt and pepper
2 tbsp extra virgin olive oil
1 tbsp butter
1 sprig fresh Rosemary

With a sharp kitchen knife take out the woody stem, then break the mushroom into eight pieces, and season to taste. Place in the heated oil in a heavy bottomed frying pan, and cook on medium heat until the bottom of the mushroom is golden (about 3 minutes). Flip over the mushrooms, and repeat. Add the butter and herbs, and baste the mushrooms in the buttery juice for a minute of two. Drain on kitchen towel and serve.

HORN OF PLENTY
Craterellus cornucopioides
Local Name: BLACK TRUMPET
Season: August–November

The French name for the Horn of Plenty is hardly an entice-
ment (*Trompette de Mort*) but this striking mushroom is a
gastronomic delight. And a harmless one. Found in broad-
leaved woodland, *Craterellus cornucopioides* is grey-black
with a deep funnel shape, and between 3–10cm in height. The
flesh is brownish-grey.

Due to its colour and habit of hiding in leaf litter, the
mushroom can be difficult to spot, but when you do find one
you will likely find more because it exists in troops, making a
basket necessary.

In the kitchen, cut in half lengthways to access the inside of
the funnel, taking care to brush out any debris and insect life.
The mushroom is strong in flavour but can be leathery in
texture, so slice thinly before adding to soups, stews,
casseroles, and wild mushroom risotto. It goes particularly
well with seafood and white fish, not least because it provides
a striking colour contrast.

JEW'S EAR   *Auricularia auricula-judae*
Local Name: JELLY EAR, WOOD EAR
Season: Throughout the year

If you go down to the woods today you'll be sure of a big
surprise if you encounter a decaying **Elder** tree: brown human
ears growing out of it. Or so it seems.

The Jew's Ear fungus derives its name from its extraordi-
nary resemblance to the human hearing apparatus, together
with the ancient belief that Judas Iscariot, having betrayed
Christ for thirty pieces of silver, hanged himself from an
Elder. The Latin name is *Auricularia auricula-judae*, meaning
'Ear of Judas', corrupted over time to Jew's Ear. Local names
include Wood Ear and Jelly Ear, the latter recognising the

gelatinous, rubbery texture of the young fungi. Age, wind and sun all shrivel the Jew's Ear – and change its colour to near black – but it is still worth harvesting when desiccated. Immersed in warm water for 10 minutes, it will rehydrate fivefold to youthful tumescence.

One of the beauties of the ugly Jew's Ear is that it is impossible to mistake for any poisonous fungus. It is also one of the very few fleshy fungi to be found all year round, from high summer to bleak midwinter. Infrequently it grows on Sycamore, **Beech**, and **Ash**, as well as Elder. To harvest, simply cut off at bark level with a sharp knife.

The Jew's Ear has little taste. Instead, it absorbs the flavour of other foods and provides texture. The fungus, with its near *Auricularia* relatives, is a staple of Asian cuisine. The trick is to shred it thinly, to reduce any rubberiness and to pierce any pockets of water. Otherwise, it spits angrily in hot fat.

Besides its use in the kitchen, Jew's Ear may have a role to play in the chemist's cupboard. The Chinese have long valued it as a cleanser of the lungs, stomach and intestines, while modern Western medicine reports the fungus as having significant anti blood-clotting characteristics, and of likely therapeutic use in combating coronary disease. There is also evidence that Jew's Ear has antibiotic and antiviral qualities. In the medieval 'doctrine of signatures' (which held, essentially, that if a plant looked like a human organ it would cure an ailment of the organ), gargles of Jew's Ears were made for complaints of the ear and throat.

To preserve, simply string on thick cotton and hang up in a warm room. Fresh Jew's Ears, kept in a plastic bag, will last up to a week in the refrigerator.

THAI-STYLE CHICKEN AND JEW'S EAR SOUP

Serves 4

Every Jewish grandmother knows that chicken soup cures all health ills; every Asian grandmother knows that ginger boosts the immune system. This Thai-inspired broth recipe is double whammy to cold and flu.

1½ tbsp cooking oil
5cm ginger, peeled and sliced into slivers
1 shallot, diced
5 large Jew's Ears
1 skinless and boneless chicken breast, cut into thin strips
1 tsp Oyster sauce
1½ tsp shoyu
1 tsp sugar
2 tbsp water

Heat up the cooking oil in a wok and stir fry the ginger strips. Add in the shallot and Jew's Ears and stir. Add the chicken strips. Stir-fry the chicken meat until browned, then add in the Oyster sauce, shoyu and sugar. Stir all the ingredients together before adding in the water. Serve with hot white rice.

MOREL   *Morchella esculenta*
Local Names: HAYSTACK, MOLLY MOOCHIER, SPONGE MOREL, MAY MUSHROOM
Season: March–May

The Morel is another mushroom sadly lacking in looks; it has a brown sponge-like head. Never mind, it is beautifully flavoursome inside, reminiscent of bacon.

The Morel is one of the most prized culinary fungi, and is expensive to buy fresh or dried. It belongs to the mushroom category *ascomycetes*, which includes the Truffle. If you are lucky and sharp eyed you may find it growing in grassy spaces in broad-leaved woods in springtime, particularly those on chalk. Not infrequently, it makes an appearance amid the bark mulch in garden borders or at the scene of extinct bonfires.

The Morel grows to 20cm high, on a stout yellowish stem, singly or in troops.

Beware of the lookalike poisonous species the False Morel (*Gyromitra esculenta*), which has a head that looks like exposed brains.

The Morel itself should never be eaten raw as it contains small amounts of toxins; these are removed by cooking.

Due to all the nooks in the cap, the Morel tends to be an ideal refuge for insects. Clean with a pastry brush. If you do not have one, slice the Morel lengthways and rinse under running water.

Morels are delicious sautéed, in sauces and omelettes, and complement chicken and fish. The caps are big enough to be stuffed. The Great War forager T. Cameron observed:

In France they [Morels] are more simply cooked by covering them with bouillon, bringing it to the boil, and allowing it to simmer for three-quarters of an hour. This method allows the flavour of the Morels full play, and I am not sure if it is not the best method of all.

STUFFED MORELS

Serves 4

The French, traditionally, stuff Morels with *foie gras*, but aside from ethical objections, the taste of the *pâté* tends to dominate. This is a vegetarian version.

100g wild rice
approx 300ml water
2 cubes bouillon
12 large fresh Morels
85g unsalted butter
6 spring onions
1 clove garlic, crushed
2 tbsp chopped parsley
25g grated Parmesan
salt and pepper to taste
2 tbsp white wine

Cook the wild rice in the water, with the bouillon. Drain.

Clean the outside of the mushrooms with a pastry brush, then cut the stem at the cap. Immerse both caps and stems briefly in salted water, and drain. Chop the stems finely, and put to one side.

Put the butter in a pan, then fry the spring onions and garlic until they 'sweat'. Mix in the rice, and add the parsley, Parmesan, salt and pepper.

Fill the Morels with as much of the rice mixture as each will hold, opening up the cap holes if necessary with a knife. Drizzle with white wine. Cover and bake at 300°C/Gas Mark 2 for about 20–30 minutes.

A lazy chef, or a chef pressed for time, might wish to stuff the Morels with a soft blue cheese such as Gorgonzola, then lay them in an oven proof dish. Then sauté the Morels' chopped stalks in butter, adding 3 sprigs of Thyme and 3 finely chopped garlic cloves and cook for a minute more. Tip in 2 tbsp of dry sherry, and let bubble until the liquid evaporates. Spread the mixture over the Morels, and sprinkle with extra virgin olive oil. Bake in a medium oven for 15–20 minutes. Serve with a bitter leaf salad.

OAK *Quercus robur*
Season: April (leaves), October–November (acorns)

The mighty Oak is so symbolic of the British countryside that a certain political party has selected the tree as its symbol. For foragers, the main use of the tree comes in autumn when it becomes festooned with acorns, which can be gathered from the tree (with a long stick) or as windfalls from the ground. The acorns, thick with tannins, are inedible raw. To remove the bitterness, Native Americans used to bury the acorns in the earth and let the bitterness leach out. Boiling achieves the same result.

In times and places of austerity, such as Germany in World War II, acorns have been roasted and ground as an ersatz coffee. Acorn coffee tastes nothing like coffee. It is, however, a perfectly pleasant beverage, something like the health food shop favourite, Barley Cup.

The acorn does seem to be a nut most valued in times of

privation. In the second century AD the Roman doctor Galen recorded poor country folk making flour from acorns.

Usually, Oaks do not produce acorns (which, botanically, are the fruit of the tree) until they are twenty, and trees are often biannual.

A light white wine may be fermented from the April leaves.

ACORN COFFEE
Boil your acorns for 10 minutes, drain, cool and shell, then place the acorns in a muslin bag and immerse in water for two weeks or more, taking care to change the water twice a week. Then dry them on a sunny windowsill, in an airing cupboard or in the oven. When the acorns are completely dehydrated, roast in the middle shelf of the oven 120°C/Gas Mark ½ for about 15 minutes. Grind. Use the acorn coffee as you would ground coffee; put into the cafetière or percolator at the rate of 2 teaspoons per cup. The acorn coffee can be kept in airtight jars or tins.

If you are tempted to make acorn flour, follow the 'coffee' recipe above but miss out the roasting stage. Keep the flour in a paper bag. Like the flour of Sweet Chestnut, it will not last long in the cupboard before going mouldy.

OYSTER MUSHROOM
Pleurotus ostreatus
Season: September–December

This is a bracket-type fungus, growing in clusters on the dead and dying branches of deciduous trees, particularly **Beech** and Poplar. The cap, which extends from 6–14cm, is grey when young and brown when old, with wavy edges that vaguely resemble those of an Oyster shell. The gills are cream.

Oyster (*Ostreatus* in Latin) Mushrooms can be found almost the year round, though make their main appearance in autumn. It is one of the few wild mushrooms to be cultivated commercially; they have little taste, but their texture is thick and firm.

Cut off the stem at the base with a knife, and wipe clean with kitchen towel or a tea cloth. Do not wash because Oysters absorb water. Try grilling the mushrooms, after first brushing in a marinade made from olive oil, lemon juice, salt and a clove of finely chopped garlic. Baste with the marinade throughout the grilling. Alternatively, deep fry them in breadcrumbs as below.

To preserve, dry or bottle in extra virgin olive oil. They do not freeze well.

Another member of the same family also makes a good meal. This is the Branched Oyster Mushroom (*Pleurotus cornucopiae*), to be found on the stumps of broad-leaves trees. The mushroom has a cream-covered cap that becomes flattened and brown with split edges in its mature state; the odour is that of aniseed. It is a very decent adjunct to meat.

FRIED OYSTER MUSHROOM CUTLETS

Serves 4

The cutlets come ready made by nature; Oyster Mushrooms grow by their own volition into cutlet shape and size.

2 large eggs, beaten
salt and pepper
1 clove garlic, crushed
¼ tsp paprika
1 tbsp finely chopped parsley
20 large Oyster Mushrooms, cleaned
plain flour
olive oil
dried breadcrumbs
1 lemon, quartered

Season the beaten eggs to taste, then mix in the garlic, paprika and parsley. One by one dip the mushrooms into the flour, then place on a plate. Pour olive oil into a large frying pan until it is about 1cm deep and heat to just under smoke point; dip the mushrooms in the egg mixture, then the breadcrumbs, then fry in the hot oil until both sides of the cutlet are golden.

Take out and place on paper towels, and press down gently with a spatula or similar to remove excess oil. Serve with a lemon wedge.

SERVICE TREE   *Sorbus torminalis*
LOCAL NAMES: CHECKER, CHEQUER, CHOKERS, LIZZORY
Season: September–October

Temptingly beautiful to look at, the brown pear-shaped fruit of the Service Tree is only palatable when it has 'bletted' – gone into a state of advanced decay following the effects of frost; then the fruit becomes sweet rather than acid, with strong overtones of sherry or plum liquor.

The Checker is a tree of ancient deciduous woodland and hedgerows, growing up to 25m high with fissured grey bark. It likes heavy clay and limestone soils, and is commonest south of Cumbria. The leaves have toothed pointed lobes, very much like those of maple. The fruits, which are 12–18mm in length, appear in September; gather in October and artificially 'blet' by storing in a cool dry place until almost rotten. Eat raw, or turn into jelly or jam. They are delicious on top of vanilla ice cream.

In Tudor times the fruits doubled up as medicine. Gerard noted the efficacy of Checkers for 'settling the colick'. Evelyn also recommended them for 'gripe'.

The country residence of the British Prime Minister, Chequers, is named after the wild Service Tree which grows in the grounds.

The Service Tree is closely related to the Common Whitebeam (*S. aria*), a wide-crowned tree of lesser stature, whose globular crimson fruit (12–15mm in breadth) is also edible. And also needs to be 'bletted'.

SWEET CHESTNUT   *Castanea sativa*
Local Name: SPANISH CHESTNUT, HEDGEHOGS
Season: October–November

Native to western Asia, Sweet Chestnuts were introduced to southern Europe by the Ancient Greeks, and brought across the Channel by the Romans. Although the tree has naturalised in Britain, the two to three kernels contained in the spiky British burr are smaller than their continental counterparts. The Sweet Chestnut, despite the name, is not related to the inedible Horse Chestnut, 'the conker tree'.

The round burr or husk of the Sweet Chestnut, which drops to the floor from October onwards, is known in some country districts as a 'hedgehog' in honour of its mass of small spines. The sputnik fruit of the Horse Chestnut is much less prickly.

With luck, a big wind and a hard floor such as a road, you may well find that the burrs of the Sweet Chestnut have smashed on landing to reveal the triangular kernels with their glossy wooden veneer. If not, step on the burrs, roll your foot briefly backwards and forwards and the kernels will be exposed. A pair of light gardening gloves can quicken the prickly matter of taking the nuts out from their casing, but cautious fingers will do. The kernel or 'nut's can be eaten raw, but this is a waste. Raw they are tough and unremarkable; cooked they are glorious.

More than a third of Sweet Chestnut kernel is made up of carbohydrate, making it a staple source of starch in some regions of southern Europe. The Italians – amongst a hundred other uses for the Sweet Chestnut – boil the kernels as a vegetable, as well as grinding them (after roasting) into flour for polenta, bread and cakes. Chestnut flour is sweet, yellow but does not rise well. The French, of course, have candied the Chestnut into *marron glacé*. In Britain, the Chestnut has tended to be viewed as a savoury, the stuff of stuffing and that Edwardian country house classic, Chestnut soup. And, of course, Chestnuts roasting on an open fire is as redolent of Christmas as cathedral choirs singing 'Good King Wenceslas', huntsmen on horses, and the Queen's Speech. If you don't have an open fire, an oven will do. Simply lay on a baking tray and roast at 200°C/Gas Mark 6. But whether you are roasting on a fire or in an oven (or indeed boiling), you must make a small x-shaped slit in the shell before exposing to heat, otherwise they explode spectacularly in a shower of Sweet Chestnut shrapnel. Boiling makes the removal of the bitterish inner skin easy to peel off.

In appearance, the Sweet Chestnut tree is large, up to 30m in height. The male yellow catkins, about 15cm long, appear mid-summer. Sometimes the tree is coppiced to produce stakes for fencing.

CHESTNUT PURÉE
Based on the recipe by Elizabeth Craig,
Cookery Illustrated & Household Management, 1936.

900g Chestnuts
50g butter
vegetable stock
75ml milk
salt and pepper
caster sugar

Cut the tops off the Chestnuts and roast them in the oven at 200°C/Gas Mark 6 for 20 minutes. Remove the outer and inner skins, and put the Chestnuts into a stew-pan with half of the butter and enough stock to cover them. Lay greaseproof paper over the top, put on the lid, and simmer for 45 minutes or so, until the Chestnuts are tender. The Chestnuts should absorb all the stock in the cooking.

When cooked, rub all through a fine sieve. Thoroughly mix this purée with the remaining butter and the milk. (You may not need all the milk, depending on how much stock has been absorbed.) Season with pepper, a very little salt, and a pinch of caster sugar. Re-warm and serve.

CHESTNUT SOUP

Serves 4

Chestnut soup used to be staple fare in country houses in winter in the Edwardian era.

675g Chestnuts
1 onion, finely chopped
1 carrot, finely chopped
30g butter
1 sprig Rosemary
chicken or game stock
150ml single cream
1 tbsp finely chopped parsley

Cut crosses in the ends of the Chestnuts, place in a pan with enough water to cover and boil for 2–3 minutes. Remove from the heat, and when the Chestnuts are cool enough to handle, peel, scrape off the papery inner skin, and put them to one side.

Sweat the onion and carrot in the butter until tender. Add the Chestnuts and Rosemary and continue sweating over a low-medium heat for 5 minutes. Pour in the stock, then simmer for 20–30 minutes. Liquidise the soup, then strain into a clean saucepan, and add the cream. Bring up to almost boiling and season to taste. Serve with a scattering of chopped parsley on top.

SWEET VIOLET   *Viola odorata*

Local Name: MARCH VIOLET
Season: March–May

Where these still grow in abundance in woodlands and shady hedgerow banks, the flowers can be picked, then candied or crystallised. Easier still, they can be added as edible decoration to salads, sandwiches, fruit salads, ice cream, banana split, biscuits and cakes.

Sweet Violet is a perennial, with kidney-shaped leaves, and

the solitary, sweetly fragrant purple flowers sit atop spindly stems up to 15cm tall. The Violet, with its seductive perfume, is the flower of Aphrodite, and accordingly is frequently made into scent for women. Rather more down home, the Romans made wine from the petals, and medieval peasants strewed them over the earthen floors of their habitations to mask unpleasant odours. Napoleon, somewhat idiosyncratically, made *Viola odorata* the emblem of the Imperial army. In herbal medicine, the petals were alchemised into soothing Oil of Violets to treat sore throats and headaches.

CRYSTALLISED SWEET VIOLETS

Sweet Violet petals
1 medium egg white
2 tsp water
caster sugar
greaseproof paper
artist's paintbrush and a pair of tweezers

Pick the Violets on a dry, sunny day. Wet petals won't candy with distinction.

Lightly beat the egg white with the water; you want a mixture like varnish not polyfilla. Using the tweezers, pick up a petal and paint over it thoroughly with the egg white mix. Make sure all parts of the petal are covered.

Now, using your index finger and thumb coat the petal evenly with caster sugar.

Place, in the shape you want, on greaseproof paper and let it dry in an airy place for 48 hours. If your rooms are cold or speed is of the essence, put the paper in a metal roasting tin and place in a barely warm oven for an hour or so. Store in airtight jars for three months.

You can use the above method as a template for the crystallising or candying of other edible flower petals, such as those of the Wild Rose.

WALNUT   *Juglans regia*
Local Names: MADEIRA NUT, PERSIAN WALNUT
Season: October–November

This native of Asia and the Balkans is now naturalised in the woodlands and parks of southern England. Underneath this spreading, deciduous tree you will find in mid-autumn the brown ripe 'hulls', which are about 5cm across; inside the hull is the nutshell, which encloses the edible, brain-looking kernel. If you are not on private ground, you can shake low branches or even shy sticks at the tree to remove the Walnuts. Store your gathered treasures in a cool dry place, or alternatively shell and keep in the freezer, where they will last for a year or more. The familiar raw nuts can be eaten whole from the hand at Christmas, chopped into cakes, biscuits, ice cream, cereals, and breakfast cereals, or coarsely grated onto blue cheese.

If you fancy doing something more exotic with Walnuts, pick the green whole fruits in July, before the shell hardens. These can be pickled in vinegar. Or made into ketchup.

Wear rubber gloves to pick green Walnuts, otherwise you will find your hands stained brown from the dye in the husk.

WALNUT KETCHUP
This is a traditional British recipe for Walnut ketchup, based on that in Mrs Beeton's *Book of Household Management*, 1861. It is essential that the Walnuts are green.

100 Walnuts
60g salt
1.2 litres vinegar
600ml port wine
20 shallots, chopped
110g anchovy fillets
1 small piece of Horseradish
2 tsp whole black peppercorns
1½ tsp mace

1½ tsp ground cloves
1½ tsp freshly-grated nutmeg
1½ tsp ground ginger
110g anchovies
500ml port

Slightly bruise the Walnuts and put into a jar with the salt and vinegar. Allow to stand for 8 days, stirring every day. Then drain the liquid from them, and boil it, with the remaining ingredients, for about 30 minutes. It may be strained or not, as preferred, and, if required, a little more vinegar or wine can be added, according to taste. Pour into sterilised bottles and seal with an air-tight lid. Store in a cool, dark place for at least a month before using.

WILD GARLIC   *Allium ursinum*
Local Names: RAMSONS, STINKERS, GYPSY'S ONIONS, WOOD GARLIC, BEAR'S GARLIC, RAMPS, MOLY
Season: March–June

You will be led by your nose to Ramsons. The garlicky smell is potent enough to put hounds off the scent of a fox should Reynard be cunning enough to run through a patch of them.

Locally common throughout Britain, Wild Garlic likes shade, damp and neutral soil, hence its affinity for deciduous woodland and thickets, where its long elliptical leaves push through the earth in dense colonies in spring. Superficially, the leaves of Garlic are similar in appearance to those of the poisonous Lily-of-the-Valley and even the Bluebell, but crush a leaf and if it smells of Garlic then it is Garlic. The single flower head, a cluster of up to twenty delicate white stars, comes later. By then, the leaves are leathery and scarcely worth the eating.

So, gather the succulent leaves of springtime, which are sublime snipped raw into butter, green salads and sandwiches (try naked, with a dressing extra-virgin oil and sea salt). They also make a useful wrap, in the manner of vine leaves. Wild

Garlic is less fierce in flavour than the cultivated variety. Sheep and cows will happily graze its glossy leaves, and even children can be persuaded to eat them.

Although, the bulb of Wild Garlic is disappointingly small it can be used in all the ways of its cultivated counterpart. Only dig up where the herb is plentiful. The widespread vernacular name Ramsons is from the Old English *hramsa*. Ramsey in Essex and Ramsbottom in Lincolnshire are just two of the places which take their name from their prolific fruiting of the herb.

Two other Garlics are to be found wild in Britain, both of them in pastureland. Crow Garlic (*Allium vineale*) has slender tubular leaves in the style of chives. It can reach up to 1.2m in height (compared to Ramsons' 20cm) and is much loathed by farmers, who may well be happy if you set to and dig up some clumps. Flowering time is June to August. Three-Cornered Garlic (*Allium triquetrum*) is an introduced species which has become naturalised in the South West. Sometimes it is called Snow Bell, in a nod to its springtime drooping white cup-shaped flowers. As with Ramsons, the odour of Garlic is the key to identification.

WILD GARLIC DOLMADES
Serves 4

80 Wild Garlic leaves
1 onion, minced
olive oil
100g cooked risotto rice
2 tsp Mint/Water Mint
4 tbsp water
1 lemon
1 tbsp tomato paste
1–2 cups vegetable stock
a little patience

Blanch the Wild Garlic leaves by dipping into boiling water for 1 minute, strain and drain.

Sweat the onion in the olive oil until translucent. Turn off the heat, but add the risotto rice and all the remaining ingredients, except for the vegetable stock, and mix well.

Put to one side.

Take 3 Wild Garlic leaves and lay side by side, so they are slightly overlapping. Put a pudding spoonful of mixture in the centre, and shape minimally into a cylinder running across the leaves. Now tightly roll the Wild Garlic leaves over the mixture – trying as you go to tuck the outer leaves over the mixture so that a small wrapped parcel is the result. When rolled, pin with a cocktail stick. If you find this method too fiddly, try laying the Wild Garlic leaves into a cross and wrapping this shape over a spoonful of mixture. The art of Dolmades-stuffing is ancient and mysterious, and not learned in a minute. So you will need patience.

Continue making Dolmades until all the mixture is used up. Using a large crock pot, or any pot with a lid, put the spare and discarded Wild Garlic leaves into the bottom as a lining. This is to stop the Dolmades burning. Pack the Dolmades in as tightly as possible, making double and even triple decks if necessary.

Spoon in about 3 tablespoons of oil and the vegetable stock. Cook on a low heat in the oven for about 30 minutes, by when the stock should have been sucked up.

The Dolmades can be dished up with Tzatziki as a starter, or placed on a bed of vegetables as a main course.

The above ingredients are all optional. Experiment at will. Haloumi cheese makes for a good binding, while beef/lamb/pork mince is traditional.

WILD GARLIC AND SPINACH FRITTATA

Serves 4

1 tbsp extra virgin olive oil
1 shallot, sliced
1 cup Wild Garlic leaves
2 cups baby spinach leaves
salt and pepper
200g fresh ricotta, crumbled
1 tbsp fresh basil, chopped
1 tbsp chopped parsley
1 tsp marjoram
10 eggs
2 tbsp Parmesan, grated
30g unsalted butter

Heat the oil in a saucepan, put in the shallot and sauté. Add the Wild Garlic and spinach leaves and a pinch of salt. Cover and cook for a minute or two, then drain to remove excess liquid.

Take the wilted leaves from the saucepan and roughly chop, then place into a bowl with the ricotta and herbs.

Crack in the eggs, tip in the Parmesan and mix. Season with pepper.

Fire up the grill to medium heat.

Now melt the butter in a frying pan, and pour in the frittata mixture and cook until the bottom has set, which will take about 5 minutes. Then put the pan under the grill to cook the top. This should take about 10 minutes. To test whether the frittata is 'done', surreptitiously insert a fork; if it comes up with liquid clinging to it carry on cooking. When the dipstick fork emerges clean of mixture the frittata is ready to serve.

WILD RASPBERRY *Rubus idaeus*
Local Names: HINDBERRY, RASP
Season: July–September

The fruits of the Wild Raspberry are smaller than those of its cultivated namesake, but worth the effort in gathering because they have greater perfume and depth of taste. They can be eaten raw, but also make jam, syrup, cordial, wine, and brandy. Young Wild Raspberry leaves harvested and dried make a herbal tea often recommended for pregnant women, since the tea reputedly acts a tonic to the uterine muscles.

The Wild Raspberry is widespread throughout Britain, but tends to be localised. Scotland would seem to be its fastness, but then about 90 per cent of Britain's cultivated raspberries are grown there, because raspberries like a cool summer. The sprawling, prickly shrub grows up to 1.5m on woods, heath and scrub. According to the Roman naturalist Pliny, the Raspberry was named *idaeus* because it grew high on the slopes of Mount Ida. Initially the fruit is green, then orange, before becoming the familiar red. Usually, it ripens before the Blackberry, and is pleasantly less thorny to rummage through in search of the fruit.

RASPBERRY ETON MESS

Serves 4

In the version traditionally served at Eton College on 4 June strawberries are used. The dish is even tastier, however, with raspberries. And easier still if you buy rather than make meringue baskets.

400g raspberries
splash kirsch
1 tbsp icing sugar
400ml double cream, whipped until soft peaks form
4 meringue baskets from a shop, crumbled

Mash the raspberries with a dash of kirsch and the icing sugar. Put in the fridge to chill for 30–45 minutes.

Whip the double cream until soft peaks form. Break the meringue into bite sized chunks. Lightly fold the broken meringues and cream into the raspberries.

WILD STRAWBERRY   *Fragaria vesca*
Season: June–August

Until the discovery of the New World, *Fragaria vesca* was the only Strawberry available in Europe. It is much smaller than its American or cultivated counterparts, and some considerable stooping or kneeling dedication is needed to pick a bowlful, let alone enough for a family meal.

The labour is worth it, because the Wild Strawberry, like the **Wild Raspberry**, is more intense in flavour and fragrance than its cultivated kin. When Doctor Butler wrote, 'Doubtless God Almighty could have made a better berry, but doubtless God never did,' he scribed for anyone fortunate enough to find this fruit. More vulgarly, after eating a sensuous Wild Strawberry you will no longer wonder why it is the fruit of Venus.

Wild Strawberries need very little doing to them. Try a little caster sugar, plus a dab of balsamic vinegar or lemon juice. And of course some cream. Should you be lucky enough to find a glut of the fruits, transform them into tarts, cordials, fools, jam, or steep them in vodka and sugar for a couple of months for Wild Strawberry vodka.

To preserve, freeze or bottle.

Wild Strawberries grow in woodland, hedgerows, in scrub and on limestone grassland. The plant's flowers have five white petals, and the leaves are trefoils with fine toothlets. Herbalists swear by tea made from leaves picked in the spring and dried; equally, old-time cooks swear by bruised leaves for meat stock, young leaves for salads.

The English name for *Fragaria vesca* is a puzzle; possibly it derives from the Anglo-Saxon 'streow', meaning strew, a reference to the way the perennial plant propagates by sending stolons in all directions, or maybe to the straw dung with which plants were manured. The great English plantsman Geoffrey Grigson suggests the derivation is from the old English 'streaw', meaning chaff, 'indicating the chaff like achenes all over a Strawberry'.

Note: Strawberries can cause an allergic reaction in some people.

WILD STRAWBERRY JAM

Makes about 1kg

600g Wild Strawberries
500g caster sugar
juice of 1 lemon

Clean the strawberries and put them into a pan with 50ml water. Bring to the boil, and simmer until the strawberries are soft. Add the sugar and lemon juice and continue simmering for about 5 minutes, stirring continuously. Test for setting by putting some of the jam onto the back of a chilled spoon. If it stiffens, setting point has been reached. If still too liquid, continue simmering for a few more minutes, then test again.

When setting point has been reached, allow the jam to cool for 20 minutes, then pour into warm sterilised jars. Cover with waxed discs and seal.

WOOD BLEWIT *Lepista nuda*
Local Name: BLUE LEG
Season: September–December

When young, the Wood Blewit is bluey-lilac all over, the 10–13cm cap becoming brown as the mushroom matures. 'Blewit' is a corruption of 'blue hat'.

The Wood Blewit, one of the last mushrooms to appear in the foraging year, can be found in woods, especially those with **Beech** stands, though it sometimes appears in troops on the garden lawn or compost heap like a hallucination. The mushroom used to be employed as a source of blue dye in the clothing industry.

Pick the whole mushroom from the ground, scraping off any dirt from the base.

The Wood Blewit has a perfume and flavour of orange, which cooking, remarkably, does little to change, making it one of the most desirable of wild mushrooms. Try in risottos, pasties, sauces and casseroles. And the Wood Blewit must be cooked, because the raw mushroom causes gastric upsets.

You will also find the Wood Blewit in gardens and hedgerows.

WOOD SORREL   *Oxalis acetosella*

Local Names: CUCKOO'S-MEAT, FOX'S MEAT, EASTER BELLS, CUCKOO'S BREAD AND CHEESE, HALLELUJAH, CUCKOO'S CLOVER, EASTER SHAMROCK, BUTTER AND EGGS, BREAD-AND-MILK, GREEN SAUCE, GREEN SORREL, WILD CLOVER, SOUR DOCK

Season: March–May

Wood Sorrel's leaves are perfect green hearts, looking for all the world as if some heavenly sculptor has carved them out of jade on the woodland floor. They usually fold down in rain and in darkness.

The lime-green leaves are lemony in taste, and give a zing to salads and stuffings for fish. Almost certainly Wood Sorrel was cultivated in days of yore; John Evelyn in his seventeenth century gardening manual, 'Plants for the Kitchen-Garden', included 'Wood-Sorrell' in his prescriptions. The Tudors and the Stuarts alternated Wood Sorrel with **Sorrel** in their green sauces for fishes from river and sea.

All that said, you may need to strip the leaves from the rather indigestible stalks before use. Since the leaves contain largish amounts of free oxalic acid, consume in moderation.

Wood Sorrel seldom grows above 10cm in height, the flowers are white and bell-shaped, and in the southern parts of the country are out to greet the cuckoo and Easter, which of course explains the multitude of country names for *Oxalis acetosella* citing the bird and the festival.

8

THE RIVER AND THE STREAM

BROOKLIME *Veronica beccabunga*
Local Names: HORSE CRESS, BIRD'S EYE, BECCY LEAVES, WATER PURPLE
Season: Throughout the year, but best March–May

This useful little plant is so overlooked that one almost feels sorry for it. It likes to grow in slow freshwater brooks and at pond edges, but will make do with any damp place. The succulent, oblong leaves are robust and fleshy, bitterer than those of **Watercress** with which it often shares a habitat. Usually sprawling, never more than 30cm in height, Brooklime has a bewitching deep blue flower, which appears from May to September. A member of the Speedwell family, Brooklime was well known in historical times as an anti-scorbutic. The Stuart herbalist Gerard advised:

Take the juice of Brook-lime, Watercresses and Scurvy-grass, each half a pint; of the juice of Oranges, four ounces; fine sugar, 2 lbs, make a syrup over a gentle fire. Take one spoonful in your Beer every time you drink to cure the Scurvy.

Of course, you could just wash its leaves and mix them in a salad. I sometimes employ it as a substitute for Watercress in the eponymous soup.

If Brooklime has its feet in water that does not freeze in

winter, the leaves will remain green all year round, making it a joyful find when almost everything is dormant or dead.

COMMON COMFREY
Symphytum officinale
Local Names: KNITBONE, BONESET, NIP-BONE, BACK-WORT, BRUISEWORT, CHURCH BELLS
Season: April–July

Comfrey is a common herbaceous perennial of river edges, ditches and damp fields. It grows up to 1m in height, with large spear-shaped leaves of noticeable hirsuteness and pink bell-shaped flowers which grow in a crook. The scent of Comfrey is reminiscent of soap and cucumber.

The occurrence of words denoting medical practice in the plant's names is testament to its long history in human first aid; 'Comfrey' itself is derived from the Latin *confevre*, meaning to grow together, which is the same meaning in Greek as the plant's generic name, *Symphytum*; ancient and medieval physicians fashioned poultices from the roots to 'knitbones'.

The Roman naturalist Pliny recorded that Comfrey was good for binding something quite different to bones: 'The roots be so glutinative', wrote Pliny, 'that they will solder or glew together meat that is chopt in pieces, seething in a pot, and make it into one lump.'

Old Pliny did not lie. Shredded Comfrey root will bind the most disparate culinary ingredients into a burger or loaf. Rural folk also used to boil the roots for wine.

But it is the protein-packed leaves of Comfrey that are most attractive to foragers. Young leaves can be steamed, sliced raw into salad, par-boiled before being added to Comfrey soup (use a white-sauce base), boiled in ever-so-slightly-salted water as a green vegetable, frittered (see opposite), or steeped in boiling water for a herbal tea believed beneficial for respiratory and gastric illnesses.

Older leaves retain flavour, but may require heroic

chomping. They used to be fed to cattle. Cut out the stems to save jaw-ache.

Comfrey is a member of the **Borage** family. Excessive consumption may lead, according to the US Food and Drug Administration, to the development of liver illnesses.

Russian or Blue Comfrey is a naturalised hybrid relic of the commercial plants that were once widely grown as cattle fodder. It differs little from Common Comfrey, other than having flowers that err to blue and a liking for roadsides rather than waterways, and is equally esculent for humans.

COMFREY FRITTERS AND PAKORAS

handful Comfrey leaves
100g plain flour
salt
1 tbsp oil
2 egg yolks
150ml milk
oil for cooking

Wash the Comfrey leaves, then dab dry with a tea towel and place to one side.

Sift the flour into a bowl with a pinch of salt. Make a well in the centre and drop in the oil and egg yolks. Gradually add the milk, whisking continuously until the batter is smooth and lump free.

Put the cooking oil in a pan no more than 2cm deep and heat to 180°C. Then dip the Comfrey leaves in the batter and fry until crispy, turning once. Serve as a snack or starter, with a squeeze of lemon.

For a more exotic, Indian, version of Comfrey fritters, make a batter using 120g gram flour, 1 tsp ground coriander, a large pinch of cumin, 2 eggs, and 3 tbsp oil. Chop the Comfrey leaves into bits, dip into the batter and make into a small ball shape. Fry in oil for a minute or two each side. Drain on kitchen paper.

MEADOWSWEET   *Filipendula ulmaria*

Local Names: COURTSHIP-AND-MATRIMONY, MAIDS OF THE
MEADOW, MEADWORT, BITTERSWEET
Season: May–September

The drainage of the water-meadows that bloomed with
Meadowsweet in the high summers of yesteryear means that
the plant's creamy, highly scented flowers are now more
likely to be found along the banks of ditches, streams and
rivers. Or on scrubby wasteland and railway embankments.
Even in 1914, when Edward Thomas' train stopped at
Adlestrop station, the sight and fragrance of Meadowsweet
caught his attention and so the plant took its place in one of
the great pastoral poems in English literature.

Mind you, growing erect up to 2m in height, with large
basal double-toothed leaves, the plant is hard to miss.

Meadowsweet is the Jekyll and Hyde plant, its two faces
caught perfectly in local oxymoronic names such as
'Bittersweet'. If the flowers smell akin to honey, the leaves
whiff of disinfectant. The plant's common English name of
Meadwort mixes both its preferred habitat and the medieval
function of its leaves in the brewing business, which was to
bitter and aromatise mead or *meodu*. Follow suit, if you will,
and chop the pungent Meadowsweet leaves in small amounts
into beer or wine, meat stews and vegetable soups.

A tisane concocted from the leaves or flowers was
frequently used in the Middle Ages to reduce fever, stomach
cramps and headaches. Not for the first time, the remedies of
old wives have been found to have a scientific foundation:
Meadowsweet was, in 1838, the first discovered source of
salicyclic acid, from which aspirin was synthesized.

Long before that, in Elizabethan England, Meadowsweet
was a popular strewing herb, engaged to perfume abodes, and
the favourite of Gloriana herself. According to the herbalist
Gerard: 'The leaves and flowers far excell all other strowing
herbes, for to deche up houses, to strowe in chambers, hals,
and banketting houses in the sommer time; for the smell
thereof maketh the hart merrie, delighteth the sense: neither

doth it cause headach, or loathsomenesse to meate, as some other sweete smelling herbes do.'

MEADOWSWEET ALE

The recipe is from Nick Weston, author of *The Tree House Diaries*, who also runs *www.huntergathercook.com* and school.

100 sets of Meadowsweet leaves
12 Meadowsweet flower heads in full bloom
12 litres water
1.25kg white granulated sugar
50g cream of tartar
15g brewer's or beer yeast

Wash the Meadowsweet leaves and flowers, place in a cauldron/very large saucepan, pour in the water and bring to the boil and simmer for 15 minutes.

Strain the liquid into a clean plastic bucket, discard the herbage, return the liquid to the cauldron and bring to the boil again. Add the sugar, cream of tartar and simmer until the sugar has dissolved, stirring occasionally.

Remove from the heat, transfer to your brewing bucket and allow to cool to blood temperature. When this (finally) happens, sprinkle on the yeast and stir well. Cover the bucket with muslin and leave for about a week, until fermentation has stopped. (If you are using a hydrometer you are looking for a reading of below 1.0000.) The Meadowsweet ale is ready after a week, but leave it for three months if you can. The alcohol content should be around 5–6%.

Serve chilled in a pint mug with a sprig of Mint.

REEDMACE *Typha latifolia*

Local Name: BULRUSH
Season: February–April (shoots), May–June (pollen), October–January (roots)

There is more to the Bulrush than providing a cradle for the baby Moses; this perennial plant is the forager's wetland dream, proving edible succulent shoots, rhizomes (roots) and flowers. There's no time of year when Reedmace – to give Bulrush its proper name – does not provide something for the table. And it is abundant and usually easy to harvest.

Look for tall belt-strap stems (sometimes reaching to more than 3m in height), with a velvety brown flower spike, at the edges of swamps, ponds, lakes and slow-moving rivers. To harvest the thick, rope-like roots which grow under water, gingerly follow the stem down into the murk with your hand and excavate some of the mud away. Then grab the root and pull up hard – either a whole root or section of root should follow. Roots are at their fullest in autumn and winter. Washed, roots can be eaten raw, though roasting in the manner of yams makes them sweeter and more digestible. Hunter-gatherers through the ages have also pounded the roots to release the starch therein in a particularly versatile, nutritious and digestible form: flour.

To make said Reedmace flour, wash and peel the roots. Cut into sections and pound (a rounded stone is ideal), put into a large china mixing bowl, add water and let steep for two or three days. Then, strain through a sieve into another large bowl and let settle. Skim off the top water, and spread the residue in a shallow dish or tin. Put in a low oven, with the door open, and heat until thoroughly dry.

The sheets of flour can now be crumbled and sieved into a fine powder.

Reedmace shoots, which grow off the tubers, can be one of the first signs of spring, bursting up with all the vigour of bamboo as early as February. Washed and stripped of their brown outer leaves, the shoots make a fresh, crunchy wayside snack, not unlike asparagus. Take them home and stir-fry in a wok, or steam like asparagus. They taste of sweetcorn. Actually, the job is better done at home because peeling off the outer layers of leaves releases a sticky jelly that requires much washing and scraping of hands. And at home, the jelly can be collected and used as a thickener like Carragheen.

There is yet more of Reedmace to be eaten. In summer the pollen is prolific enough to be collected and used like sugar. Cover the top, male, flower with a carrier bag, tighten around the bottom of the spike with your hand and shake. Be careful not to snap the stem; if you do, the female flowers below will not develop seed.

WATERCRESS
Rorippa nasturtium-aquaticum
Local Names: CREESE, WELL-KERSE, RIB
Season: March–October

In Victorian Britain, Watercress was hawked on the streets of cities as a vegetable. Sellers were young children. One eight-year-old girl, 'pale and thin with privation', told the sociologist Henry Mayhew how she collected the Watercress from Farringdon market between four and five of the morning, then:

When we've bought a lot, we sits down on a doorstep, and ties up the bunches. We never goes home to breakfast, till we've sold out. I go about the streets with the water-creases, crying, 'Four bunches a penny, water-creases.'

She would be lucky to get a penny for her four bunches, because in summer 'there's lots [of Watercress], and 'most as cheap as dirt.' The poor ate it in sandwiches for breakfast.

Watercress' role as cheap fodder for the grimy proletariat did it no favours in the fashion stakes, and it steadily fell from culinary grace in Britain. Even so, Watercress was run in to London's Covent Garden as late as the 1960s, when Dr Beeching cut the branch railways. By the 1970s, if Watercress made an appearance on a table, it did so as a garnish with overcooked beef in garish chain restaurants.

Thankfully, Watercress has been rehabilitated and is a fixture in the cuisine of People Like Us. A perennial (sometimes annual) plant of water margins, of shallow streams and ditches, Watercress is fixed by its root system, while the hollow stems allow the upper branches and glossy green, elliptical leaves to float. The leaves will retain their colour even in winter. From spring to summer, Watercress produces clusters of small white flowers carried on the stem tips. There is only one harmful plant with which it can be confused: *Apium nodiflorum*, Fool's Watercress, which has umbels of flowers *down* the stem.

To harvest, cut off the leaves and stems at or below the water-line with a sharp knife or dress-making scissors, since pulling disturbs the delicate root system. Against the usual rules of foraging, the mature, darker leaves are the ones to cherish, because they have more taste. The prefixes in the plant's Latin name, *Rorippa nasturtium*, mean 'nose-twister cress', and you will want the peppery fieriness to pep up salads or perk up a cheese sandwich. In both these cases, the plant is eaten raw.

There is, however, a caution to eating Watercress *au naturel*. In slow-moving water to which livestock has access, or into which farm effluent runs, the plant can harbour the liver fluke *Fasciola hepatica*, which can parasitize humans.

So, the one safe way to eat this tasty and nutritious plant – it has more calcium than milk, more folic acid than bananas, more vitamin C than an orange – is to cook it. It can be blanched or steamed as a green vegetable, or it can be stir-fried. But its pungency is enjoyed to prime cooked advantage in Watercress Soup.

In some floras and herbals, Watercress is listed as *Nasturtium officinale*, the *officinale* tag recognising the plant's value to the apothecary. Since the beginning of recorded time, society has lauded the healing properties of Watercress. Hippocrates, in 400 BC, situated his first hospital beside a stream so he could grow Watercress to feed his patients; the Greeks also believed that Watercress improved the workings of the brain, hence the Greek proverb: 'Eat Watercress and get wit.' Meanwhile the Cretans considered the semi-aquatic plant an aphrodisiac, and the Romans used it to treat the mentally ill. A millennium later, the twelfth century mystic Hildegard von Bingen advised the consumption of boiled Watercress water for curing fever and jaundice. Almost another millennium on, research at the University of Ulster discovered that Watercress acts in a similar way to chemotherapy in the killing and inactivating of cancer cells.

WATERCRESS SOUP

Serves 4

large bunch of Watercress
30g butter
1 tsp lemon juice
570ml vegetable stock
4 medium-sized potatoes, cubed
150ml milk
salt and freshly ground black pepper

Chop the Watercress. Melt the butter in a heavy saucepan and lightly fry the cress together with the lemon juice for 5 minutes. Pour in the vegetable stock, together with the potatoes. Simmer until the potatoes are tender (about 10 minutes). Liquidise in a blender. Return to the saucepan. Add the milk and seasoning. Stir. Reheat until the soup is just under boiling.

The soup can be served hot, but also cold, as a British wild food larder version of gazpacho. A pinch of paprika on top will set it off perfectly.

WATERCRESS PESTO

1 large clove garlic, peeled
1 tsp capers
1 tbsp pine nuts
40g grated Parmesan cheese
170g Watercress
4 tbsp extra virgin olive oil
lemon juice
salt and black pepper

Put the garlic, capers and pine nuts in a food processor and whizz. Add the Parmesan cheese and Watercress and blend until the Watercress is shredded. Add the olive oil and a squeeze of lemon juice. Whizz again. Season to taste.

WATER MINT   *Mentha aquatica*
Local Names: BISHOPWEED, HORSE MINT, BISHOPWORT, LILAC FLOWER
Season: April–October

'The savour or smell of Water Mint,' wrote Gerard, 'rejoiceth the hart of man for which cause they strowe it in chambers and places of recreation, pleasure and repose.' Tread on this perennial and you will understand what Gerard meant: an intoxicating aroma rises up to the nose.

Found in sprawling clumps throughout Britain on the banks of ponds, streams, lakes, rivers, swamps, marshes and anywhere determinedly damp, Water Mint has given its name to Minety in Wiltshire, and Minstead in Hampshire. The aerial stems reach 90cm, and the small lilac flowers, clustered onto terminal heads, appear in July. Before then gather the rough, oval, dark green going on purple leaves, taking from the top of the plant where the leaves are the most tender.

The taste of Water Mint is harsher than that of the garden's Common Mint, but can be used for all the same sauces, chutneys, cold drinks and Moroccan-style teas. Add to new potatoes, to peas, to yogurt, make into Mint julep and Mint liquor. Do not dry the leaves, because they will not hold their flavour when desiccated. Preserve in oil or vinegar.

Mint, of course, does more than taste good, and is much recommended in both traditional and alternative medicines for the treatment of digestive problems.

There are some 15 other Mints to be found growing wild in Britain, all of them edible and drinkable and trailing the distinctive menthol smell. Apple Mint (*M. suaveolons*) is excellent in salads. Pennyroyal (*M. pulegium*) is the one that should not be picked, not because it is harmful to humans, but because it is rare.

MINT AND PEA SOUP

Serves 4

2 shallots, chopped
55g unsalted butter
800g frozen peas
500ml chicken or vegetable stock
1 bunch Water Mint leaves, stripped from stems
salt and pepper
100ml crème fraiche

Fry the shallots in the butter until soft. Add the peas, stock and Mint leaves and simmer for 10 minutes. Transfer the ingredients to a food blender, and blend until smooth and lump free. Pour back into the pan, season, and add the crème fraiche. Reheat until just bubbling, then serve immediately.

WILD CELERY *Apium graveolens*
Local Name: SMALLAGE
Season: May–August

Wild Celery was used to crown the victors of the Greek Nimean games, held to honour Zeus. The pragmatic and epicurean Romans, meanwhile, exploited the herb's culinary properties; the leaves, mixed with dates and pine kernels, made a standard stuffing for suckling pig during the empire.

Since Wild Celery is the ancestor of cultivated celery, you can pretty much do anything with the former that you would do with the latter. The stems, leaves and seeds of the wild version, however, are stronger in taste and texture. Try grinding the seeds and adding to salt to make celery salt or putting some finely chopped leaves in milk when poaching fish. Soup and Wild Celery are a kitchen love affair. Stir chopped leaves into vegetable stews during the last 5 minutes of cooking (to retain both flavour and nutrients) or use the stems to make a piquant wild version of celery soup.

The leaves, gathered in summer, are easy to dry, and are useful in flavouring dishes from stocks to stews to stuffings.

Wild Celery is not the easiest of plants to identify. Aside from rivers, ditches and marshes, it grows besides the seaside and will reach 60cm in height. Stems are solid, the leaves are fan-shaped and loosely toothed, and the tiny white flowers are borne in a compound umbel. Your nose may detect the plant before your eye; the aroma of celery is distinct.

9

THE COAST

DULSE
Palmaria palmata/Rhodymenia palmata
Local Names: DUILEASG, DILLISK
Season: Throughout the year, but best March–May

Dulse is a flat reddish-brown seaweed, with a single blade that divides into five or so fingers looking very much like a giant upturned hand, or 'palmata', of up to 50cm in length.

Before the days of convenience foods, coastal dwellers would eat Dulse as a snack, or masticate it like chewing gum to pass the time. The Irish took the tradition of chewing Dulse with them to America, where bags of it dried – it dries particularly well – were sold on street corners of the 'little Irelands' in Boston and New York. A commercial Dulse industry still exists in Ireland; 'champ', a dish in which Dulse simmered in milk is beaten into mash potato, is a staple of Eire's cuisine.

Dulse can be picked the year round in the land between low and mid tide, but is most succulent in spring. The seaweed's distinct notes of iodine and salt lend themselves especially to soups. Dried in the sun or oven in chunks it makes a healthy nibble for children.

Pass it around at drinks parties instead of peanuts and crisps. Pan fry as 'chips'. When dried and ground up, it can be used in place of salt and monosodium glutamate.

When harvesting the seaweed, don't pull it off from its

discoid 'holdfast'. Instead, cut off some of the straps and leave some behind.

For a vegetable, Dulse has a significant protein content, as much as 20 per cent of its weight.

Pepper Dulse (*Laurencia pinnatifida*) is also worth gathering. This most unusual looking red seaweed, with small branches that look like rounded tridents, is to be found on rocky shores and in rock pools. It is hot to taste, whence comes its name, and makes an excellent pickle and a condiment.

DULSE AND POTATO ROSTIS

Serves 4

400g desiree, charlotte or vivaldi potatoes, grated by hand
300g Dulse, washed in cold water
250g milk (optional)
1 onion, finely chopped
pepper
3 tbsp olive oil
fresh chives

Dry the grated potato with a clean hand towel to remove moisture.

Simmer the Dulse in water or milk until tender, about 10 minutes. Drain and roughly chop.

Mix the chopped Dulse, onion and grated potato together in a bowl with a sprinkle of pepper.

Heat the oil gently in the frying pan, and add heaps of the potato mixture and flatten into cakes.

Cook over a low heat for about 10 minutes, making sure the rostis are browned on the bottom. Turn over the rostis carefully, and cook on the other side for a further 10 minutes. Serve garnished with chopped chives.

FENNEL   *Foeniculum vulgare*
Local Names: SPIGNEL, FINKLE
Season: March–June (leaves and stems)
October (seeds), September–February (root)

Fennel is not indigenous to Britain, but has forsaken the medieval herb garden and gone native. It grows in abundance on the south coast, but you'll find it near old houses and on wasteland too in the rest of the country.

Growing up to 2m in height with stiff, vertical stems, Fennel can look disconcertingly like dill or the deadly Hemlock. The salient clue to Fennel's identity is the aniseed smell the fine leaves give off when crushed.

It tastes of anise too. The whole of the plant is edible. Pick the young feathery leaves throughout the spring and early summer, and add to salads and sauces, or use as garnish. Flowers and stalks can all be used to do what Fennel has historically done best, which is to flavour fish. Gut fish, stuff with Fennel, and grill. Alternatively, make a Fennel sauce and cover the fish, or steam Fennel and make a bed for the fish. The prevalence of Fennel beside the seaside is serendipitous to say the very least.

Compared with cultivated Fennel, the bulb root of wild Fennel is untidy, small and fibrous, and you may reasonably decide to ignore it. More practical in the kitchen are, in addition to the leaves, Fennel's pungent seeds. Collect the heads of the seeds in late summer, while they are still green, and dry at home by spreading out on white paper in a warm place. When fully dry the seeds can be put in an airtight container, where they will keep for a year or more. Use like the Italian and French do, to flavour breads, savoury biscuits and soup.

Stalks can also be preserved by drying, as can leaves, by the simple expedient of cutting off branches in summer and hanging upside down in a dry, light airy place. Freezing, however, retains more of their flavour. If you do decide that the bulbs are worth the digging up, they will keep for weeks in the fridge after a good scrub clean.

'Foeniculum' means 'little hay', in reference to the aroma of the herb when dried.

FENNEL SAUCE

Fennel sauce particularly suits oily fish, as the herb acts as a 'refresher'. By far the easiest Fennel sauce to make is to chop a tablespoon's worth of Fennel leaves and add to melted butter. Serve immediately, otherwise the sauce becomes discoloured.

A more sophisticated version is:

1 shallot, chopped
15g butter
150g chopped Fennel leaves or ground Fennel root
150ml vegetable or fish stock
1 egg yolk
1 tbsp crème fraiche

Take a saucepan and sweat the shallot in the butter. Add the Fennel to the pan and stir enough to cover with butter. Pour in half the fish stock, cover and simmer until the Fennel is cooked, about 15 minutes. Place the pan contents into a blender with the remainder of the stock and whirl until a smooth paste is obtained. Return to the saucepan. Before dishing up, mix the egg yolk with the crème fraiche and stir into the sauce with enough heat underneath to make 'piping hot'.

The sauce is good for almost all fish. It will perk up the most anodyne Pollack, and bourgeoisify the coarsest Coley.

EASY FENNEL SHORTBREAD

Makes 15–20 biscuits

500g plain white flour
200g caster sugar
375g unsalted butter, cut into small cubes
1 heaped tbsp dried wild Fennel seeds,
  crushed in a mortar and pestle

Put everything into a food processor and briefly blitz until a dough is formed.

Roll into a log and refrigerate for 1 hour.

Cut into rounds 1cm thick and sprinkle with caster sugar.

Bake at 180°C/Gas Mark 4 for 10 minutes. Cool on a wire rack.

KELP *Laminaria digitata*
Local Names: OARWEED, TANGLE, SEA TANGLE, HORSETAIL KELP, FINGERED KELP
Season: Throughout the year, but best April–June

To go gathering Kelp, take a billhook or a large pair of biceps. Kelp has a 2cm tough stalk, the roots of which attach to rocks with a claw or holdfast, leaving you the choice of cutting with a steel hook or playing tug-of-war. If neither method appeals, wait for a storm; Kelp is frequently washed up on beaches.

Common on all the rocky coasts of Britain, sometimes in 'Kelp forests', this olive-brown seaweed has a distinctive leathery, broad blade divided into fingers; together blade and stalk can reach 3m in length. Harvest in spring and early summer.

Washed and chopped finely, the blade makes a tangy contribution to salads, fish stews and seafood soups. Usefully, it thickens as well as flavours.

To preserve Kelp, wash in fresh water and leave to dry outside in the sun. Dried Kelp can be ground into a flour or powder. Powdered Kelp is a standard dietary supplement for people and pets, not least because of its high iodine content. Formerly Kelp and its relative Sugary Kelp (*L. Saccharina*) were the only sources of the chemical. Both Kelps also have a long history in agriculture, being used as fertilizer, and in industry, as a source of soda and potash for the making of soap and glass.

LAVER   *Porphyra umbilicalis*
Local Names: RED SEAWEED, SLOKE, PURPLE LAVER, SLABHACAN
Season: Throughout the year, but best March–June

Porphyra umbilicalis is the seaweed that forms the base of the Welsh breakfast delicacy 'Laverbread', or *bara lawr*.

Abundant around the coasts of Britain, Laver is a greenish reddish plant that browns with age; the flat membrane-like frond, which extends to 25cm in length, is divided into lobes with wavy edges. Gather from middle shore down to the low tide mark from rocks and groynes, and wash briefly in seawater to release any trapped marine life. Carry home in a plastic bag, and wash again, at least twice, this time in fresh water.

Laver is best harvested in spring and early summer, but can be taken throughout the year. The seaweed is extremely nutritious, rich in vitamins A, B, B_2 and C, protein, and a variety of minerals. Its high iodine content gives it a flavour like that of olives.

Fresh fronds make a tasty and unusual wrapper for baked fish, and Laver can be added to fish soups as a flavoursome thickener. Or, it can be puréed, and served on toast as 'The Welshman's Caviar'. (For instructions on puréeing see the Laverbread recipe opposite.) On his walking tour through Wales in the 1860s George Borrow was much taken with the dish of 'moorland mutton and piping hot Laver sauce'. In other parts of Britain it was washed, boiled, and made into a salad with the addition of oil, vinegar, salt and pepper.

When put into sterilised jars, Laver purée will keep in the

fridge for several days. Alternatively, place in plastic food bags and stick in the freezer.

LAVERBREAD

Conveniently the recipe for Laverbread also provides the general method of preparing the seaweed. First thoroughly rinse the seaweed, then place in a heavy-bottom saucepan filled with cold water. Bring to a simmer, then cook for anything up to six hours (taking care to stir with a wooden spoon and top up as necessary), until the Laver has broken down. Strain well, then use a blender to turn the Laver into a dark green paste.

This slimy, sea-smelling paste is Laver 'caviar', along with being the base for Laver sauce, soup and Laverbread. To make Laverbread:

200g Laver purée
50g fine oatmeal
white pepper
2 tbsp olive oil or bacon fat

In a bowl, mix the Laver purée and the oatmeal until thoroughly combined. Season with white pepper and place in the fridge for 20 minutes.

Then with damp hands, break off golf-ball sized pieces of the Laverbread mixture and flatten into small patties about 2cm deep.

Heat the oil or, better still, bacon fat, in a pan over a medium heat. Fry the patties until they are golden brown, about 3 minutes each side.

Serve immediately with fried Cockles and bacon.

LAVER SOUP (CAWL LAFWR)

Serves 4

75g butter
1 large onion, peeled and chopped
3 medium potatoes, peeled and chopped
1 medium carrot, chopped
75g Laver purée
1.2 litres fish or lamb stock
½ tsp sugar
salt and pepper
chopped parsley for garnish

Melt the butter in a saucepan, add the chopped vegetables and cook until they start to brown. Stir in the Laver purée and the stock, bring to the boil and simmer until the vegetables are tender, about 25–30 minutes. Allow to cool slightly, then liquidise. Return to the saucepan, add the sugar and seasoning to taste. Bring to simmering point. Pour into bowls and garnish with the chopped parsley. Serve with warm crusty bread.

For a vegetarian option, substitute vegetable stock for the fish or lamb stock.

LAVER CRISPS

Pretty much any edible, flat seaweed will make crisps, but beware of the spitting as the seaweed fronds release stored water during frying.

Wash and dab dry the Laver in a tea towel. Cut the Laver into pieces about 5cm square. Put enough sunflower or olive oil (at least 2cm) in a high sided frying pan to deep fry the Laver and heat. Put in the Laver in batches and dry until crisp.

Remove with a slotted spatula and drain on kitchen towel.

Season with sea salt and chilli flakes.

LOVAGE   *Ligusticum scoticum*
Local Names: SEA LOVAGE, SCOTS LOVAGE, SEA PARSLEY
Season: April–October

A perennial Umbellifer reaching 1.5m in height, Lovage is common on the sea cliffs of Scotland and Northern Ireland. With its large, glitteringly green leaves and dense clusters of yellow flowers it is a strikingly handsome plant, with a powerful celery flavour. So use sparingly.

The culinary uses of Lovage are many. Leaves can be used to make soup, or added whether fresh or dried to soups and salads. Better still, wrap the leaves around fish for baking. In times of famine in Scotland, the leaves were used as a vegetable to keep scurvy at bay. But it makes a poor dish of greens.

Young stems – which are hollow – can be steamed, or candied like Angelica.

To gather the seeds, wait until they are yellow-brown, then cut off the stems and hang the heads upside down in a paper bag. The ripe, dry seeds will fall to the bottom of the bag. In Mediterranean countries, Lovage seeds are crushed to flavour bread. Equally, they can be sprinkled on salad, mashed potato, Welsh rarebit and cauliflower cheese.

The thick brown root is also aromatic. Grated root adds savoury flavour to salads. Peel before grating.

The cultivated form of Lovage, *Levisticum officinale*, is frequently encountered playing truant from the garden on wasteland.

MARSH SAMPHIRE   *Salicornia europaea*
Local Names: GLASSWORT, SALTWORT, JOINTED GLASSWORT
Season: July–September

At low tide a bed of Samphire on a mudflat is a hallucination, a verdant stranded lawn. Samphire is no less exotic close-up, and does a decent impression of a miniature succulent bonsai. It is not to be confused with **Rock Samphire**, a cliff-dwelling member of the Goosefoot family.

About 10cm tall by the end of July, Samphire is to be found on saltings almost everywhere around Britain. I have picked it in the Ynyslas estuary in mid Wales and in the Salcombe estuary in Devon, though I fancy it is most common in East Anglia. The best Samphire is washed by the tide. You should cut the plant, rather than uproot it, since Samphire roots stabilize the local eco system. It is also the law. By the end of August Samphire begins to turn yellow in advance of self-seeding. At this advanced age a plant may be 45cm in height.

When you get your Samphire home, wash under a running tap to remove detritus. Young Samphire can be eaten raw as a nibble, but those who like their food hot will wish to eat in the traditional manner. Tie bundles of Samphire together and boil briefly, and serve with warmed olive oil or melted butter. To eat this 'Poor Man's Asparagus' pick a stem by the root end and scrape the flesh away with your teeth.

Samphire starts to 'melt' almost as soon as it is picked and will not keep for more than a day without preservation. Traditionally it was pickled, or served as green sauce for mutton.

One of the local names for Samphire is 'Glasswort'; until the nineteenth century Samphire, which has a high soda content, was gathered commercially for use in glass-making.

PICKLED SAMPHIRE

600g washed Samphire
500ml cider or white wine vinegar
1 tsp peppercorns
1 tsp Juniper berries
2 bay leaves
100g white sugar

Wash the Samphire in fresh water. Place all the ingredients in a large saucepan of boiling water and cook for 10 minutes. Leave to cool. Take out the Samphire and insert lengthways into a 1kg sterilised preserving jar. Pour in the liquid and close the lid.

No salt is needed because Samphire is salty enough. I prefer the above method of pickling Samphire because it is light on vinegar. If you prefer the traditional way of Samphire-pickling, boil the Samphire in water, drain, insert in the jar, add the spices, sugar, bay leaves and fill to the neck with vinegar.

ROCK SAMPHIRE *Crithmum maritimum*
Local Names: SAMPER, ROCK SEMPER, SEA SAMPHIRE
Season: May–June

No relation, despite its name, to **Marsh Samphire**. For centuries, Rock Samphire was one of the most sought-after vegetables, and was big money; barrel-loads of the perennial Umbellifer were harvested on the coast, preserved in sea-water, and sent up to London; it is this plant that Shakespeare means when he writes about the foragers precariously descending the cliff at Dover. Yes, Rock Samphire is delectable, but not so delectable it is worth risking your life for. Seek it not on the cliff face; try the bottom, on rocks, on shingle and sometimes it can even be found growing on a sandy beach.

At 50cm in height, with hairless stems and fleshy grey-green succulent fingers, Rock Samphire looks like a sprawling emaciated cactus. The smell is distinctively sulphurous. Pick leaves and snip stems before the dullish yellow flowers appear in umbels. Do not take too much from one plant.

Very young leaves, washed, can be chopped raw into salads, if you like a piquant peppery taste. Traditionally, leaves were boiled or steamed as greens, or pickled. The Tudor herbalist Gerard considered: 'The leaves kept in pickle... is a pleasant sauce for meat, and stirreth up an appetite to meat.' He might have added that it is pleasant on fish too. Try garnishing fish dishes with *Crithmum maritimum*. Better still, make a wild food tartare sauce with it.

'Samphire' is derived from the French herbe-de-Saint-Pierre, St Peter being the patron saint of fishermen.

ROSEMARY *Rosemary officinalis*
Season: Best June–September

Rosemary means 'dew of the sea', and the coast is one of the prime habitats of the herb, although you will also find it growing in graveyards, and near the entrances to old cottages, where it was planted because of its association with remembrance. Introduced to Britain by the Romans, Rosemary is a perennial growing to about 2m in height with masses of needle-shaped leaves, green above, grey below. The tubular flowers, which appear in May through to August, are blue and tucked into the leaf joints.

To harvest the leaves, snap them sideways. They can be dried, but fresh Rosemary is best. They are at their most flavoursome when the plant is in flower and higher in essential oils.

The pungency of Rosemary allies the herb with the roasting of meat and potatoes. Sprinkle on top of lamb, pork, and rabbit, potatoes, or push sprigs inside chicken. A scattering of Rosemary in roasted vegetables gives a Mediterranean twist. Strew Rosemary on BBQ charcoal to produce an aromatic smoke. Very finely chopped leaves – which are decidedly chewy in their natural state and shape – can be added as flavouring to marinades, jellies, and sauces.

Rosemary was much praised by practitioners of herbal medicine for its antiseptic qualities and the Greeks lauded its ability to improve memory. Scholars would wear garlands of Rosemary when sitting exams. Recent scientific research has confirmed that the herb does indeed boost cognition.

Traditionally in Britain, Rosemary was used to make a herbal ale. The word 'bridal' comes from the 'bride ale' made from Rosemary given to the woman in white at her wedding ceremony. To make it, follow the instructions for **Hop** Beer, adding the needles from 15–20 stripped sprigs of Rosemary at the same time that the malt extract enters the process.

SCURVY GRASS   *Cochlearia officinalis*
Local Names: SCROOBY GRASS, SCREEBY
Season: April–June

'Officinalis' is the label accorded to plants judged by the apothecary to be of medicinal use. Gerard lavishly praised Scurvy Grass in his *Herbal* for its ability to rid sailors of scurvy, 'this filthie, lothsome, heavie and dull disease... in which the gums loosed, swolne, and exculcerate: the mouth griviously stinking'. Deficiency in vitamin C, however, was not peculiar to the diet of matelots on long sea voyages, and land dwellers also suffered from scurvy into the Victorian era. Scurvy Grass leaves, and a tonic prepared from them, were sold around city streets, the vendors crying:

> *Hay'n Wood to cleave,*
> *Will you buy any scurvy Grasse?*
> *Will you buy any Glasses,*
> *Ripe St Thomas onions?*

By all accounts Scurvy-juice was bitter medicine. By the mid Victorian era, Scurvy Grass had dropped from use in favour of citrus fruits and another hawked green vegetable, **Watercress**.

Common on coastal cliffs and saltmarshes throughout Britain, excepting the English Channel, this low spreading biennial or perennial plant (typically 30cm tall and 50cm wide when mature) can also be found inland on mountains, even by the side of roads where salt from gritting has run off. Several smooth stems spring from the rootstock, bearing leaves that vary between kidney and heart-shaped.

Scurvy Grass is strong and acrid in taste. Gather leaves in spring, and add sparingly and raw to salads and sandwiches, or use as garnish.

SEA BEET   *Beta vulgaris subsp. maritima*
Local Names: WILD SPINACH, SEA SPINACH
Season: March–September

Sea Beet is the wild founder of the dynasty of cultivated spinaches and beets we eat, turn into sugar, and give as fodder to farmyard animals. Even the red tubular Beetroot is a direct descendant.

The plant grows prolifically round the coasts of southern Britain, producing large thick green leaves, that are sometimes veined, from January onwards. Flowers are small, greenish and borne on a spike. Some specimens of this bushy perennial reach over 80cm in height and 50cm in width. To harvest, cut off the leaves at the base of the stalk with a sharp knife.

Use in the kitchen as Spinach, remembering that the leaves of Sea Beet are fleshier and more leathery; only the youngest leaves near the top of the plant will serve as salad, and even then they may keep your jaws fit. Older leaves near the base of the plant will require the tough midrib and larger veins to be stripped out. When cooking the larger leaves, boil with a little water in the bottom of the saucepan for 2–3 minutes. Try them with a poached egg on top.

On the Isle of Wight, Sea Beet was traditionally eaten with pork or bacon; in other coastal areas, the vegetable was served as soup. More modern twists on Sea Beet see it as an ingredient in aloo sag, stir fries, and folded into pancakes.

SEA BUCKTHORN   *Hippophae rhamnoides*
Local Names: SALLOW THORN, WYWIVVLE
Season: September–October

The orange berries of this deciduous shrub look good enough to eat. And are. Unhappily, they are protected from eager fingers by vicious spines. The ripe berries, to the forager's further frustration, tend to burst on touching. Most Sea Buckthorn recipes, however, only require the juice of the berries so a small DIY contraption will save heart and finger ache: fit a metre or so of plastic tubing to a plastic funnel. Hold the funnel under a bunch of Sea Buckthorn berries, press the berries into the funnel with a potato masher. The juice will run down the tube into your collecting container. Failing that, and if Sea Buckthorn is locally plentiful, you might prune off some berry-laden branches and take home. Put in the freezer overnight. Next day the berries will shake off easily.

Sea Buckthorn juice is one of the true superfoods in the wild food larder, and in Russia and Asia has been dispensed as a tonic for thousands of years. Genghis Khan's armies marched on it. A study published, rather more recently than the Mongols' heyday, in *Food Research International*, suggested why: Sea Buckthorn berries are crammed with vitamins A, K, E, C, B_1 and B_2, fatty acids, amino acid, lipids, organic acids, carbohydrates, folic acid, and flavonoids. The taste of Sea Buckthorn alone acts as a pick-you-up: it bursts with a tart, sour vitality due to its high concentration of malic acid – the stuff put in sour 'extreme candy' for kids.

Sea Buckthorn is common on dunes and the upper shore, especially on the east coast of England; there are stretches of Wales and Scotland where it is rare or absent. You'll also find it planted by roadsides in gardens by conservationists and designers. It is an easy plant to identify, even when not in fruit, with its narrow silver-grey leaves similar to those of Willow and, topping 3m, it is hard to miss. The bush's scientific name stems from the Greek for 'Glittering Horse', because the plant's leaves were fed to racing horses. According to legend, Sea Buckthorn leaves were also the favoured fodder of Pegasus.

The uses of Sea Blackthorn juice and berries are many and varied. They can be used to make jams, pies, sauces for game, marinade for mackerel, baked with apples, and to flavour champagne and schnapps. Sea Buckthorn went off the British menu some centuries ago, but is making a comeback in uptown restaurants. The flavour is strangely moreish.

Beware, though, the smell of cooking Buckthorn berries is not nice. Rabbit intestines smell better. Open the windows. Fortunately the odour does not transfer to the cooked product.

SEA BUCKTHORN SORBET

If you have picked berries, rather than using the cheaty method of obtaining juice advised above, you'll need to extract the juice from your fruits first. Do this by putting 400g of fruit in a pan, adding 50ml water, and bringing to the boil. Turn down the heat, then simmer for 20 minutes. Press the resultant pulp through a sieve. To extract yet more juice pour a little hot water from a kettle over the pulp and mush. Repeat if necessary until you have 400ml juice. Throw away the pulp and seeds

200ml water
200g sugar
400ml Sea Blackthorn juice

Pour the water and sugar into a small saucepan and bring to the boil. Reduce heat and simmer for 5 minutes to make a syrup. Allow to cool.

Mix the Sea Buckthorn juice and sugar syrup and churn in your ice cream maker according to the instructions. If you don't have an ice cream maker, stick the ingredients in a blender and blitz until you have a soft paste. Put in a plastic airtight container and place in the fridge until it hardens.

SEA KALE   *Crambe Maritima*
Local Names: SEA CABBAGE, COLEWORT
Season: April–June

Sea Kale is a member of the cabbage family, which is reflected in its French name *chou marin*. It grows wild along the shore, on shingle banks, and on cliffs. The summer-flowering heads are white, the leaves long, flat and fleshy with wavy edges.

But it is the spring shoots the forager looks out for. Often these are blanched naturally by sand creeping over them, but from time immemorial coastal folk have heaped pebbles on top of the young plants so they grow in darkness. This not only de-bitters the Sea Kale, it elongates the edible stem and the nascent head.

Cut the shoots just below sand level with a sharp knife, between April and June, when they are between 12–15cm high. Be stingy with yourself, leave some shoots for the plant, some for other people to eat. Sea Kale is uncommon, and in northern Scotland it is absent. One reason for Sea Kale's scarcity is that the Victorians, who had a craze for the plant, stripped whole coasts bare.

To cook, place the stems in boiling salted water until tender (about 10 minutes). Serve with melted butter, grated Parmesan, dash of lemon juice. Or Hollandaise sauce.

Two other brassicas grow in much the same salt-sprayed places and are worth taking. Black Mustard (*B. nigra*), a 1m high annual, which produces a mass of yellow flowers in late spring; in autumn the fruit pods contain a much sought-after seed that can be ground up with vinegar to make a 'hot' condiment. The seeds may also be fried and added to curries. Don't overlook the leaves, which can be blanched as greens or added to salads.

Wild Cabbage (*B. oleracea*) is the ancestor of all the cultivated European brassicas, from broccoli to Brussels sprouts, that grow in the back garden and the allotment. The yellow flowers appear in a spire in late spring, and the flesh, greyish-green leaves are, well, cabbage-shaped. Wild Cabbage, also called Sea Cole and Sea Cabbage, is nationally scarce. If you do encounter it, take off only a few young leaves in spring. It is more strongly flavoured than its cultivated heir, being acrid like kale. To make a Wild Cabbage meal fit for a king, roll up the leaves into a sausage shape, and slice across with a knife. Fry the green slices in olive oil, with a dash of shoyu, stirring to prevent burning. Serve with a hint of lemon juice and fried bacon piled on top.

SEA LETTUCE   *Ulva lactuca*
Local Names: GREEN LAVER, OYSTER GREEN
Season: Throughout the year

The name of this seaweed is unimaginative but accurate; *Ulva lactua* does indeed look like green lettuce, though a rather bedraggled one as it clings to rocks, groynes and other seaweeds below the high-water mark on shingle beaches. Common on all the coasts of Britain. Cut from its moorings with a knife.

Sea Lettuce can be prepared as true **Laver**, although more coarsely seaweedy in taste. Since the plant is high in protein, fibre, chlorophyll, antioxidants, vitamin A, vitamin B_1, iodine and other essential minerals, it is worth making some dietary use of. The Japanese and Scandinavians put it in soups and chowders. Try it in stir-fry. At the very least the leaves, which extend to 20cm across and 18cm in length, make a good wrap for baked fish.

Sea Lettuce at least has a name that is slightly enticing, which could not be said of its relative Gutweed (*Ulva intestinalis*). Neon green and extremely common on every British coast, Gutweed makes food for many migrating geese. It is edible by humans, although it is tasteless and requires copious washing in cold water to remove sand trapped in its grassy fronds. Perhaps best dried and used as a condiment.

SEA PURSLANE   *Atriplex portulacoides*
Local Name: SHRUBBY ORACHE
Season: Throughout the year, but best April–May

If nothing else, you have to admire the tenacity of Sea Purslane, which forms grey shrubby carpets on the side of estuaries and salt marshes, places most plants would eschew.

The evergreen plant's leaves are oval, small, no more than 2cm in length, and mealy-covered with silver undersides; as one would expect of a plant growing in such harsh conditions, they are swollen, succulent and saline.

So, quite nice then as a tangy, crunchy addition to salads, sandwiches and stir fries – if gathered when they are young. The leaves, matt and silvery, make an unusually attractive and tasty garnish. Historically, Sea Purslane was boiled and served up as a side vegetable, but even a rigorous 10 minutes being superheated is unlikely to reduce Sea Purslane to a texture acceptable to the modern palette. Liquidised, the leaves can form the basis for a green sauce for fish.

Sometimes listed in floras as *Halimione portulacoides* or *Obione portulacoides*, Sea Purslane was formerly grown as a pot-herb, for the use of its young leaves in the kitchen and in the medicine cupboard. Dispensed by the village herbalist, Sea Purslane was said to cure everything from protruding navels to excessive libido.

Sea Purslane is a tempting wayside nibble, but if gathered from the wild it would likely benefit from careful washing.

SHELLFISH
Season: Traditionally, when there is an 'R' in the month

I do not believe, as some foragers do, that Shellfish are akin to plants because their lack of mobility means they can be 'picked'. Shellfish are fauna, and when you gather them you are taking the life of a sentient being. And no-one who has tried to catch a Razor Clam as it scoots under the beach can be under any apprehension that Shellfish are stationary.

It follows that Shellfish should be dispatched humanely. Therefore, after cleaning them, place them in the freezer, where the cold makes them dormant. Then plunge into boiling water.

There are a few obvious rules to follow in gathering Shellfish. Never collect Mussels, Cockles, Winkles or other Shellfish from any place where effluent or industrial pollution is discharged into the sea. Always ensure you wash any Shellfish before eating. Also be absolutely certain that the Shellfish you collect is alive. If you eat a Shellfish that has been dead for even a very short period, you are very likely to end up in hospital. Cockles and Clams live in the sand and you cannot be sure that they are alive unless you dig them out. Winkles live on rocks, and need to be prised off. Mussels should be over 45mm long with closed shells, and linked to others by the seaweed on which they live.

Mussels are not the only Shellfish with a 'Minimum Landing Size'; this, however, can vary from coast to coast, so check with the local authority.

Infants, children, pregnant and breastfeeding women, and elderly adults, as well as those with any medical conditions such as diabetes, should not eat raw Shellfish.

That said, Shellfish have been gathered by humans for millennia, and are one of the tastiest and healthiest forms of protein on the planet, being low in saturated fats.

Almost all Shellfish are edible. Below are listed the seven you are most likely to find, are safe to eat, and whose conservation status is good enough for you to gather with a clear conscience.

CLAM *Mya arenaria*
Local Names: NANNY NOSE, PISS CLAMS, SAND GAPER,
STEAMERS, LONG NECK

'The Poor Man's Oyster' has a flattish hinged pale-grey shell up to 13cm across, buries itself in sand and mud, sending up a siphon to the surface to draw in seawater that is filtered for food; an excurrent siphon expels the used water. To discover whether Clams are present, look for round holes in the surface of the beach or estuary at low tide. Alternatively, tread back and forth, because the pressure causes the Clams to eject water from their siphons. Dig down with a children's beach spade until the shell is found – it may be 20cm down – and finish off with your fingers so as not to damage the shell.

If you are certain of the water quality, are not squeamish and aren't in one of the categories listed on page 160, you can down the Clam raw, like an Oyster. Otherwise, place in a shallow tray containing seawater for a day to allow the Clams to clean themselves. Do not leave the Clams for longer than this; they will either drown or foul the water.

To kill the Clams humanely follow the advice on page 160. Boil for 15 minutes, discard any that do not open, and trim off the sheath which surrounds the siphons. Remove the flesh and boil, bake or fry. If you are feeling inhumane, steam open in a little water, olive oil, glass of white wine and chopped garlic clove.

While you are out hunting 'Sand Gapers', keep an eye out for its close relative the Surf Clam (*Spisula solida*) which is abundant almost everywhere. No-one would accuse it of being flavoursome, but it does bulk out a bouillabaisse. The Hard Shell Clam is an American import – allegedly dumped from a transatlantic liner in Southampton Harbour – and, growing to more than 10cm, requires only a handful for a meal. But if it's the caressing of your taste buds you desire, seek the Palourde (*Tapes decussates*), which is sweet meat.

Generally, Clams do not have a Minimum Landing Restriction.

CLAM CHOWDER

Serves 4

A standard recipe from New England, Clam chowder central.
Americans call *Mya arenaria* the Soft-shelled Clam.

40 small Clams
100g smoked streaky bacon, cubed
1 clove garlic, crushed
2 shallots, chopped
25g butter
1 small tin sweetcorn, drained
250g potatoes, cubed
1 lemon
275ml milk
275ml double cream
1 bay leaf, chopped
salt and pepper
1 tbsp chopped parsley

Wash the Clams, then put them in a large saucepan with 1
cupful of water. Cover tightly and cook on high heat. As soon
as the Clams open, drain the Clams into a colander over a
bowl. You need to retain the Clam liquid. When the Clams
have cooled, remove from their shells and cut up the flesh into
1cm cubes.

In a heavy-bottomed pan fry the bacon, garlic and shallots
in the butter just enough to soften them. After 5–10 minutes
add the Clams, Clam liquor, sweetcorn, potatoes, squeeze of
lemon and stir. Pour in the milk and cream and bring just up
to the boil. Add the bay leaf and simmer gently for 45
minutes, then gently mash the potato to make the sauce
thicker. Continue simmering for 10 minutes. Season. Pour the
chowder into a tureen, garnish with chopped parsley.

Over in New England, they like to serve Clam Chowder
with cream crackers broken into the soup.

COCKLES   *Cerastoderma edule*

Cockles thrive all around the coast of Britain, living about 5–6cm below the surface of tidal flats. Look for small holes, often with a piece of green seaweed attached, when the tide has gone out.

Dig up with a children's seaside spade, your bare hands, or a metal garden rake. The shell of the Cockle is fluted ribbed, up to 6cm across, and usually creamy-grey. Leave any Cockles that are less than 2.5cm wide. Wash off in seawater, then place in a shallow tray of saltwater for a day. Wash under running fresh water before ending their lives.

Cockles take only 5 or so minutes to cook in boiling water. Discard any that do not open.

Minimum Landing Restriction: From none to 23.8mm. Permits needed in some areas.

LIMPET   *Patella vulgata*

Limpets are single-shelled molluscs which cling to rocks in exactly the way their name suggests. To gather these conical Shellfish – in French they are *chapeau Chinois*, or Chinese hat – you need a sharp knife with a pointed tip to prise them off. An element of surprise also helps; any Limpet aware of a predator will use its internal muscular 'foot' to intensify the suction by which it holds fast to its resting place. Limpets use the foot to travel in search of algae and seaweed on which to graze, but always return to the same resting place. At low tide, the Limpet survives because of saltwater retained inside the shell. A mature Limpet may reach 6cm across.

After gathering, place in a tray of saltwater overnight, or for eight hours maximum. Then plunge into clean fresh water, to remove the taste of salt.

Limpets have been eaten for thousands of years – their shells have been found in prehistoric middens in the Orkneys.

To prepare Limpets for a recipe, boil them for 2–3 minutes after which the 'meat' will come loose from the shell. Strain off the liquid, and remove the shells; if any Limpets have not abandoned their homes, prise them out with a large needle.

Pull off the head (and, if you wish, the black guts) of each individual Limpet, which will now be ready to cook. Limpets are legendarily chewy, so traditionally they are added to stews and cooked into submission. But the loveliest Limpets I have ever eaten have been those fried in a little butter, pepper and vinegar over an open fire on a beach in west Wales.

Minimum Landing restriction: None.

MUSSEL *Mytilus edulis*
Local Name: BLUE MUSSEL

In all likelihood, this is the most common edible Shellfish in the northern hemisphere. Mussels are bivalves, meaning they have double-hinged shells; these shells are oval, blue-black, and reach 10cm in length. Must Mussel beds are 'laid' by local fisherman as a commercial enterprise, and should be ignored; there are still many rocks and jetties where you will find wild Mussels attached by their thread 'beards'. Look for Mussels without barnacles.

After gathering, put in a tray of slightly salted water overnight. Before cooking, wash under running water, and check that the Mussels are alive: those that are safe to eat have closed shells, or shells that close immediately when tapped. Discard any open or cracked Mussels, or any that float during cleaning. Scrape off the 'beard' with a knife.

The meat of the cooked Mussel should be a creamy yellow and almost fill the shell. Cooking Mussels can be as simple as this: steam for 4–5 minutes in a saucepan with a close-fitting lid. Only a small amount of water is needed, as the Mussels will release their own liquid as they cook. Discard any Mussels that do not open. Thus cooked, the Mussels can be added to other dishes, or scoffed immediately.

Minimum Landing Restriction: None to 51mm. Be aware that some Mussel beds are commercially owned and managed.

MOULES MARINIÈRE ET FRITES

Serves 4

This classic French dish actually varies from seaside region to seaside region in France. If a 'richer' soup is required, cream can be added in the fashion of the Normandaise.

2kg Mussels
1 packet oven chips
4 shallots, chopped
2 cloves garlic, chopped
55g butter
1 tbsp chopped fresh parsley
150ml dry white wine
150ml water
salt and pepper

Clean the Mussels as on page 164, and put the chips into the oven. They should cook in the same amount of time as the Moules, 25 minutes.

Sweat the shallots and garlic in 15g of the butter in a large saucepan for 10 minutes. Add the parsley, wine and water (in that order) and cook for 5 minutes. Put in the Mussels, put on the lid and leave to steam on a low-medium heat, stirring gently with a wooden spoon once or twice, until the shells open. This will take about 5 minutes.

Then put a colander on top of a saucepan and tip in the Mussels. Throw away any of the Shellfish that have not opened. Boil the Mussel liquid well until reduced. Stir in the remaining butter, season to taste.

Transfer the Mussels to a tureen, pour over the marinière sauce and sprinkle with the parsley.

Eat with the chips. The au fait way to extract the Mussels from their shells is by using an empty Mussel case (there are bound to be several in which the meat has become detached in cooking) as a pincer to pull the fish from the others.

A British culinary twist on the French moules marinère is to cook them with **Alexanders**. The recipe is by Andy Hamilton of *www.theotherandyhamilton.com*.

Serves 4

60 Mussels
1 onion, chopped
30g finely chopped Alexander leaves
60ml parsnip wine
60g butter
black pepper to season

Clean and prepare the Mussels as on page 164, then put them in a very large saucepan with the onion and half the Alexanders. Pour in the parsnip wine, and heat to steam them open. Slowly over the next few minutes each Mussel will open; discard the ones that don't. Pour into a colander and collect all the juices.

Pour the juice back into the saucepan leaving about one tablespoon in the bowl, this last bit often contains grit. Heat and bring back to the boil whisking in the butter.

Put the Mussels into a big bowl then pour the juice over them adding the rest of the Alexanders and a few twists of black pepper.

OYSTER *Ostrea edulis*
PACIFIC OYSTER *Crassostrea gigas*

According to the Victorian sociologist Henry Mayhew, the population of London consumed 124 million Oysters a year. One consequence of the Victorian mania for Oysters is that *Ostrea edulis* is now a scarce species outside a few strongholds in Scotland, the Solent and Ireland. Moreover, where the Oyster does occur it is likely to be living in a private Oyster bed and in Scotland it belongs to the Crown anyway. It is also a creature that prefers to abide below the low-tide line.

But if Oysters are your fancy and you live in the south of England, look out for the Pacific Oyster (*Crassostrea gigas*). This is an invasive species, more than 10cm long, enjoying the warming of the seas – and can be picked without qualms. Take a heavy chisel to prise them off, purify them in slightly salted water for 1–2 hours (after that they will drown), and, unless you have an Oyster 'shucking' knife, take out the Shellfish with a short, strong knife. Wrap the Oyster in a tea towel – they have edges like cut glass – place down on a hard surface with the beastie's hinge pointing towards you. Insert the knife into the small hole in the hinge and twist until the shells snap apart. Then run the knife blade backwards along the upper shell to sever the muscle that holds the two shells together. Carefully move the top shell, and remove the black beard. The Pacific Oyster is quite big to eat raw, but you can try if you are game and absolutely certain that the water was lovely.

Oyster: Minimum Landing restriction 70mm diameter.

Pacific Oyster: No Minimum Landing Restriction.

BLOODY MARY OYSTERS

Serves 4

An entrée, or an *amusement de bouche*.

12 Pacific Oysters, opened

For the Bloody Mary mix:
2 tsp lemon juice
pinch celery salt
2 tsp Tabasco
2 tsp vodka
2 tsp Worcester sauce
300ml tomato juice

Mix the Bloody Mary ingredients together in a jug and chill. Put the Oyster on a shot glass. Cover with a dash of the Bloody Mary mix – and down in one.

GRILLED OYSTERS

Serves 4

24 Pacific Oysters, removed from shells
melted butter
chopped parsley
freshly grated Parmesan cheese
6 tbsp toasted breadcrumbs
cayenne pepper
150ml single cream

Pre-heat the grill.

Clean the bottom shells of the Oysters, then dry them.

Mix together the butter, chopped parsley, Parmesan, breadcrumbs, and a small sprinkling of cayenne. Pour a teaspoon of the cream into each bottom shell and replace the Oyster. Then dot each Oyster with the butter and herb mix.

Grill until lightly browned, about 3–4 minutes.

RAZOR CLAM   *Ensis ensis, Solen marginatus, Ensis siliqua, Ensis arcuatus, Ensis americanus*

Strictly, there are four native species of Razor Clam, but the difference in looks is so subtle as to be meaningless if you are hungry.

Razor Clams are so called because they are long and blade-like, the spitting image of the cut-throat razor wielded by Victorian gentlemen. The largest reach 20cm and can live upwards of twenty years. They are common almost everywhere on the British coastline, with the exception of parts of the east coast of England, and Devon and Cornwall. An invasive American species inhabits The Wash, Essex and Kent.

Look for Razor Clams on sheltered, gradually sloping sandy beaches and estuaries at low tide, both at the water's edge and at paddling depth in the sea. Razor Clams live in vertical burrows which leave a tell-tale 'keyhole' opening in the sand above; they may further betray their presence by throwing up a jet of water.

How to get the Razor Clam out of its lair? The time-honoured methods of catching Razor Clams are those described by T. Cameron:

They burrow deep, but may be induced to come nearer the surface and thus cut off with a spade by dropping a pinch of salt into the key-holes. They may also be captured by thrusting long hooks into their shells and pulling them to the surface. He who would catch razors, however, must learn to tread softly, and to stand perfectly still when he is over their laces of retreat.

At the merest sniff of trouble, the Razor Clam can up-end itself and disappear away through the sand like the proverbial knife through butter.

In part of Scotland, Razors are caught by 'spooting', slowly walking backwards over wet sand and looking for the appearance of air shafts and digging the creature out frantically. Applying salt from a plastic tub or bottle is the least gory and least back-breaking method. When the Razor Clam rises like an apparition, grab it to prevent it retreating and then gently pull it up. The 'foot' will still be anchoring the Shellfish in its home, and if you tug violently the animal will be pulled apart.

The Razor is arguably the most satisfying Shellfish to gather. They are sizeable, have a complex flavour that is simultaneously salty and sweet, and their texture is like that of tender squid. Transport them home in a wet beach towel.

There is a national commercial Minimum Landing Size for Razor Clams, which is 10cm in length and which should obviously be honoured by foragers.

To eat: quickly wash under running cold water, then lay them on a baking tray under a hot grill for a minute or two. This will prompt them to open their shells. Remove the Clams and leave to cool. As soon as they can be handled, take out the Clam and with a pair of kitchen scissors snip off the black tip of the 'neck' and the brown bits near the 'foot'; in doubt, remove anything that is not white. Put back in the shell and return to the grill for another 2 minutes of cooking.

Less is best with Razor Clams. In France, they are grilled in the shell and served with a last-minute dollop of hot garlic butter and sprinkling of chopped parsley.

If grilling Clams does not appeal, plunge them into boiling water for one minute, then prepare as above when cool. Dry, dip in egg and breadcrumbs and flash fry, no more than 30 seconds each side. Serve with a dash of lemon juice.

WINKLE   *Littorina littorea*
Local Name: PERIWINKLE

These small Sea-snails, no more than 30mm high, are native
to the coast of the North Atlantic. At low water, search for
their whorled shells – not unlike a Mr Whippy ice cream – in
pools amongst the rocks and the shingle at the bottom of the
beach. They come in a variety of colours, from green to
brown, though are predominantly black. Leave the smallest,
gathering only those about 2.5cm across. Live Winkles will
either be clinging to a hard marine surface, or moving with a
slimy trail in its wake like a Garden Snail. Children, armed
with a pail, make great Winkle sleuths.

Put the gathered Winkles in a tray of slightly salted water
overnight to clean them. To cook, plunge into boiling water,
turn down the heat and simmer for 5 minutes. Take out the
Winkles, allow to cool, then remove the black trap-door cap.
Insert a needle into the opening, and if the flesh can easily be
'winkled' out the Winkle is cooked. The taste is almost
impossible to describe. Like liquorice? Nuts?

Like other Shellfish, Winkles are high in protein, low in fat.
Use in seafood soups, or serve up in the traditional Winkle-
stall manner, with a sharp malt-vinegar dressing. They are
toothsome enough to eat on their lonesome, on a piece of
buttered bread. If you are feeling inventive or foreign, boil
them in a French court-bouillon (see **Snails**), or cook in the
Dutch manner, hot in a Garlic Mustard sauce. The Scottish are
said to have eaten Winkles in porridge.

10

THE HILL AND THE HEATH

BILBERRY *Vaccinium myrtillus*
Local Names: WHORTLEBERRY, BLAEBERRY, COWBERRY, CROWBERRY, WIMBERRY, HURTS, WHORTS, HEATHERBERRY, BLUEBERRY
Season: July–September

Bilberry grows on moors, heaths, wood-edges where the soil is acidic. The 6mm blue globose berry is sweet, high in vitamin C; one bite and you will know that the Bilberry is related to the American blueberry.

The only snag with Bilberry is that the shrub grows no more than 60cm tall, meaning that the gathering of the fruit requires some stooping unless you hail from Lilliput. This is especially true on windswept mountains, where the small, much-branched shrub huddles down even lower. Often the berries are hidden under the oval, finely toothed leaves, so you will have to look hard for them. In many European countries a special day was set aside for harvesting the berries, which was the nearest Sunday to 1 August; in Ireland, this was known as *Domhnach na bh Fraochan*, Fraughan Sunday, when whole communities would make a day of picking Bilberries with rush baskets. The savvy also took a wooden comb, otherwise the Bilberries have to be picked individually. Miners across in Britain, meanwhile, ate Bilberries by the score in the belief that the fruit offset the toxic fumes of the coal pits.

Bilberries make good eating just by themselves, or raw with cream. If enough can be gathered, they can be mixed in fruit salads, cooked in fruit tarts, made into jam, put into jellies and traditional English summer puddings. They also make a heavenly sauce for game. In northern Europe, where the Bilberry crops prolifically, the fruit is used to make wine.

BILBERRY SUMMER PUDDING

Serves 6

This is an easy version of English Summer Pudding using Bilberries.

1000g Bilberries
175g golden caster sugar
6–8 slices white bread
pinch ground cinnamon

Simmer the Bilberries and sugar in 150ml water for 10 minutes, stirring occasionally. Meanwhile, cut the crusts off the bread, then sprinkle the slices lightly with cinnamon. Line a pudding bowl with cling film (this enables an easy turn out of the pudding), place slices of bread in the bottom so they overlap and completely cover the bowl; you'll need to squidge and cut the bread with scissors to do this. Then pour in a third of the stewed Bilberries, add a layer of bread slices (again cutting to ensure a fit), then repeat twice, ensuring you have a good bread seal uppermost. Put on a side-plate, and weigh this down with a full cans of beans or similar. Chill overnight in the fridge. Turn upside down. Serve with whipped cream.

If you don't have Billberries, make with Blackberries or any mixture you can gather of edible wild berries.

BISTORT   *Polygonum bistorta*

Local Names: EASTER MAN GIANTS, EASTER LEDGES, POOR MAN'S CABBAGE, EASTER GIANTS
Season: March–May

In the Lake District Bistort is known as 'Easter Man Giants', which is likely a corruption of 'Easter *mangeants*'. The narrow leaves of Bistort do indeed generally appear in upland damp meadows in time to be eaten at Easter. Traditionally Bistort leaves were stuffed, or boiled with leaves of Ramsons, Dandelions and Nettles, before being compressed in a basin as a 'spring pudding'. Served with an egg perched on top, the spring pudding was believed to purify the blood. An 'Easter Beer' made from Bistort was a 'health tonic', poured down the throats of generations of country kids.

You can, as you might suppose, more simply take advantage of Bistort's virtues by dishing up the plant as greens. It needs very little cooking.

Disappointingly, Bistort is tricky to distinguish in spring, when it is edible. Look for triangular leaves on an unbranched stem. By summer, when the Bistort shows off its terminal pink floral spike, its levels of tannic acid are so high that you won't want to eat it.

Bistort is now rare in the south. In the west and north, especially on the hills, it remains common. Redshank (*Polygonum maculosa*) is Bistort's poor cousin, the habitué of wasteland and arable fields.

BOG MYRTLE   *Myrica gale*
Local Names: GALE, CANDLEBERRY, MOOR MYRTLE, GOLD-WITHY, SWEET WITHY, SWEET WILLOW
Season: Throughout the year

Bog Myrtle bushes grow (up to 1.5m tall) with abandon in boggy ground, where their resinous fragrance can scent the air, particularly in late spring. At first sight, Bog Myrtle looks like a miniature willow, which explains the local names which riff on 'Willow' and 'Withy'. Flowers are very small, reddish, in catkins at the tips of shoot, and appear in June–July. In the days of yore, Bog Myrtle was cut for bedding (reputedly it kept fleas away), as insect-repellent, as yellow dye, as perfume for linen, wax (from the fruit catkins) for candles, styptic for wounds, and, above all, for the making and flavouring of ale with its lance-shaped leaves. The Vikings used Bog Myrtle in the potion they brewed before going 'beserk' in battle. On a more peaceful note, before the Reformation, Bog Myrtle from the Highlands was supplied to the monasteries for their breweries.

The very bitterness of Bog Myrtle that enamoured it to brewers sacred and profane means that the plant's role in the kitchen is limited to spicing up meat in the manner of a bay leaf. If the drinks cabinet is more your realm of interest, infuse gin with it. Or, you might try Bog Myrtle ale.

This recipe is by Ceres:

You need enough of the small tough leaves almost to fill a crock. Pour water over them till they are covered, then strain it into a pan and add half a pound of honey to each gallon. Bring to the boil and then pour this sweetened water back over the leaves, pushing them well down with a wooden spoon or old-fashioned wooden potato-masher.

Add more boiling water to top up, so that the leaves are covered, but without any more honey, and then let it all stand until it is only warm. Stir in the yeast gently until the water starts frothing. Let all this stand and 'work' for six to eight days, then de-froth it and strain it off into a cask. Do not cork the cask, until the ale has stopped 'working', and do not try any bottling unless you have strong stone jars. It is not fit to drink until it has stood for at least a month, or more if the weather is warm.

The Old English name for Bog Myrtle, *gagol*, has entered numerous place names, including Galsworthy in Devon.

CLOUDBERRY   *Rubus chamaemorus*

Local Names: BAKED APPLE, SALMONBERRY, YELLOW BERRY, BAKED APPLE BERRY, EVRON, NUB, KNOUTBERRY

Season: June–August

If you are tramping the high moorlands of Scotland, Wales and northern England, the Cloudberry will be one of your few wayside snacks.

The Cloudberry is a small hardy perennial, at most 25cm tall, with wrinkled, kidney-shaped leaves; only female plants produce the red berry which ripens to amber in the late summer to look like an individual orange Raspberry sent from heaven.

Eat neat, but if you find the seeds heavy chewing, stew it, pie it, or boil it with sugar to make into a golden marmalade. The Finns like to serve Cloudberries with cheese, while the Norwegians blend it into whipped cream to make the pudding 'Multekrem'. The taste of Cloudberries is as exotic as the berry's appearance, tart, musky, exotic and with a hint of apple (the Americans call Cloudberry 'Bakeapple').

The derivation of Cloudberry is from 'clud', the Old English for hill; the local names Nub and Knout also mean hill.

There are other berries to be discovered high on the moors and heaths, but aside from the Cloudberry and Bilberry they are of limited interest. The Black Crowberry (*Empetrum nigrum*) makes fine food for birds but hardly inspires the human palate, while the Red Cowberry (*Vaccinium vitis-idaea*) and its close relative the Cranberry (*Vaccinium oxycoccus*) are acidic and best utilized in the making of jellies to accompany game and poultry.

CLOUDBERRY SAUCE
Delicious poured over vanilla ice cream.

200g Cloudberries
3 tbsp caster sugar
2 tbsp fresh orange juice

Mash the berries, then pass through a strainer to remove the seeds. Put in a food processor with the sugar and orange juice, and whizz until 'saucy'. Use hot or cold.

HEATHER   *Calluna vulgaris*
Local Names: HADDER, LING, GRIG, HEATH, MOUNTAIN MIST, GRIGLANS
Season: July–September

In the uplands of Britain, Heather used to be fuel, bed, thatch, orange dye, sweeping broom, ale – and its flowers, dried, made into tea (drunk without milk), sweet wine and ale.

Common throughout Britain on heaths and bogs, as well as on misty mountains, Heather is an evergreen shrub with narrow scaly leaves growing no taller than 60cm; the pink bell-shaped flowers, rich in nectar, appear in summer. Bees feeding on Heather make a dark, fragrant honey. In herbal medicine, Heather 'bells' are used as an anti-diuretic and anti-septic.

Robbie Burns allegedly supped a 'Moorland Tea' in which Heather was added to the flowers and leaves of **Wild Strawberry**, **Bilberry**, **Blackberry**, Speedwell and **Wild Thyme**.

Another poet, Robert Louis Stevenson rhapsodied about 'Heather Ale':

From the bonny bells of heather
They brewed a drink long-syne,
Was sweeter far than honey,
Was stronger far than wine.

Heather Ale, or 'Fraoch Leann', is one of the most ancient beverages known to humankind; on the Isle of Rhum a Neolithic shard discovered by archaeologists contains traces of a fermented drink made with Heather. Even more than whisky, Heather Ale has a claim to being the national drink of Alba; and it was probably the 'magic potion' the Picts imbibed before warring with the Romans.

HEATHER MEAD
1.5kg clear, wildflower honey
1.5 litres boiling water
125ml dried Heather flowers
sweet mead yeast
1 tsp yeast nutrient

Equipment (sterilised before use)
large saucepan/cauldron
4.5 litre demijohn
airlock and bung

Pour the honey into a large saucepan, using some of the hot water to rinse any residual honey out from the jars. Add the remainder of the hot water and stir energetically to dissolve the honey.

Put the Heather into the bottom of the demijohn and pour over the honey liquid. Top up with cold water if necessary. Allow to cool to room temperature, put a hand securely over the top of the demijohn to cover the opening and shake vigorously. Sprinkle in the yeast and yeast nutrient.

Place the airlock and bung into the top of the demijohn.

After eight weeks, remove the Heather and rack. Then rack again at six months. Bottle when fermented out. Leave for a year before drinking.

JUNIPER *Juniperus communis*
LOCAL NAMES: BASTARD KILLER, AITEN, MELMONT
Season: October–February

There are over sixty Juniper species, but the one which yields edible fruits in Britain is *Juniperus communis*. Evergreen, prickly, usually a sprawling shrub but sometimes a 6m conical tree, Juniper is commonly found on chalk downs and clay hills. The pea-shaped berries are green before ripening into blue-black in their third autumn. Immature and mature berries are invariably found existing side by side.

The berries, which are mealy, aromatic and tart, are famously added to gin as flavouring. Indeed, 'gin' is a corruption of the Dutch *genever*, meaning Juniper. Unfortunately, Juniper berries are almost wholly neglected in English cooking, although their savoury spiciness suits both meat and vegetables. Add a level teaspoon of crushed fresh berries to pâtés, sauerkraut, green cabbage, marinades for meat, game casseroles, and game pie. Or rub over the surface of roast pork, pigeon or venison. Juniper makes game more 'gamey'. The berries can be dried, then stored for months in an airtight bottle. They can be made into a herbal tea too, though perhaps only if the Apocalypse comes and all other herbal teas are eradicated.

One useful guide to the identification of Juniper is the apple-like fragrance the needle-shaped leaves give off when crushed. Women who are pregnant, wish to become pregnant, or who are nursing a child should not eat Juniper fruits. The Juniper has the country name of Bastard Killer. The berries are strongly diuretic.

ROWAN   *Sorbus aucuparia*
Local Names: MOUNTAIN ASH, WICKEN-TREE, QUICKBEAM
Season: August–September

Rowanberry jelly is the wild stuff to serve with game and lamb; intriguingly orange-red in colour, with a somewhat bitter undertaste, it rings the changes on the ubiquitous Redcurrent jelly.

The Rowan is a slender deciduous tree reaching about 15m in height, with distinctive leaves which are alternate and divided into pairs of leaflets. In the summer the tree produces berries which are yellow but turn orange then a tantalising scarlet in autumn – but do not follow the example of the birds and eat them raw, because in this state they are mildly poisonous. They need to be cooked before consumption. As well as jelly, berries can turned into syrup, soup, and wine.

You will find Rowan trees on the mountainside, in woods and in urban areas, where it has been intentionally planted for its delicate beauty and benefit for wildlife. In its mountain fastness, it is almost always the highest tree to be found, with perhaps just a windblasted, bowed over **Hawthorn** for company.

ROWAN JELLY

1.5kg Rowan berries
1.5kg Crab Apples
approx 500ml–1 litre water
a jelly bag
1kg (at least) sugar

Rowan has a low pectin content, so needs the addition of Crab or green apples to make it set.

Remove the berries from the stalks and wash. Peel and chop the apples, leaving in the pectin-rich cores.

Place all the fruit into a large cauldron along with enough water to reach halfway up the fruit. Bring to the boil, then simmer, mashing and stirring occasionally with a wooden spoon. When the fruit is reduced to a very soft pulp (use a potato masher if you like), tip the mixture into a jelly bag (or sieve lined with muslin) suspended over a bowl, and leave to drain. As with similar jellies, if you want a clear jelly let it drip of its own accord. To hasten the process but cloud the jelly, squeeze the pulp.

Measure the juice in a measuring jug, then transfer it to a clean pan and add 450g sugar for every 600ml of liquid. Stir over a low heat until the sugar has dissolved, then boil rapidly, skimming off any scum, until you reach setting point – it's 106°C. If you don't have a sugar thermometer, boil brutally for ten minutes, take the pan off the heat and drop a little of the jelly onto the back of a refrigerated spoon. If the jelly blobs, it is ready; if it runs, return to heat and boil for another 5 minutes, then repeat the test. As soon as setting point is reached, pour the jelly into warm, sterilised jars. Cover with a disc of waxed paper, then screw on a lid. Leave for at least a fortnight before eating.

To make a 100 per cent Rowanberry jelly you will need to add at the simmering stage pectin bought from a shop. The jelly should keep for up to a year.

SPIGNEL   *Meum athamanticum*

Local Names: BALDMONEY, WILD FENNEL, BAWD'S PENNY, HOUKA, MEU, BAWD MONEY, SPIKINEL, SPIKNEL
Season: August–October

This plant grows on high pasture-land, especially in the Highlands of Scotland. Aromatic, with finely divided leaves, flat white-purplish heads from June onward, Spignel is a member of the carrot family, and its somewhat sweet and spicy roots – reminiscent of Angelica – were eaten by upland communities until recently. The leaves may be dried and used as a herb, the seeds likewise.

The local name Baldmoney is a corruption of Balder, who was the Apollo of northern Europe. The writer 'BB' gave the name Baldmoney to one of the gnomes in his children's classics, *The Little Grey Men* and *Down the Bright Stream*.

Culpeper enthused about Spignel thus:

Is under the government of Mercury in Cancer, and is an excellent plant in disorders of the stomach from phlegm, raw cruder humours, wind and relaxations, pains, want of appetite and digestion, belching, fuctations, loathings, colic, gripes, retention of urine, and all obstructions. It is a good pectoral and stomach carminative warmer. The root expels wind, urine, and the menses; is good in hysterics, green-sickness, catarrhs, grieves, and facilitates generation. The root powdered and given with loaf sugar, and a glass of its infusion in white wine or beer, or water taken evening and morning for some days, mostly brings down the menses and lochia, facilitates the expulsion of birth and after-birth, and eases a windy colic after many more pompous and promising things have failed. The roots should be gathered when the leaves begin to put forth in the spring. The seed is rather stronger, and answers the same use as the root. The leaf is used outwardly in baths, poultices, and fomentations with success, where the skill of the physicians has done no good.

SPRUCE FIRS
Picea abies, Picea sitchensis et al
Season: March–May

Spruce trees are not native to Britain, having been introduced here from the sixteenth century onwards. They are the most widely planted of trees, being commonly grown in parks and gardens as ornaments, as well as on plantations for their wood. Spruce Firs have linear evergreen leaves; the most familiar is the Norway Spruce (*P. abies*), better known as the Christmas Tree.

Spruce 'beer' was widely brewed in colonial America and Canada as a beverage to accompany food and friendship, and as a tonic and anti-scorbutic. Soldiers and sailors were daily doled it.

SPRUCE BEER

This old method for making Spruce Beer was recorded in Thomas H. Raddall's *Halifax, Warden of the North*, 1948:

Take 7 pounds of good spruce and boil it well till the bark peels off. Then take the spruce out and put in 3 gallons of molasses and boil the liquor again, scum it well as it boils, then take it out of the kettle and put into a cooler. When milk-warm in the cooler put a pint of yeast into it and mix well. Then put it in the barrel and let it work for 2 or 3 days, and keep filling it up as it works out. When done working, bung it up with a tent-peg in the barrel to give it vent now and then. It may be used in 2 or 3 days.

A more modern version is:

22.7 litres water
handful wild Hops
750g fresh outer twigs of Spruce tree
3kg sugar
1 tsp ground ginger
ale yeast

Put the water, Hops and Spruce twigs into a large cauldron. Boil vigorously for 30 minutes.

Strain the liquor into a fermentation bin, add the sugar and ginger and stir vigorously. Leave to cool to blood temperature. Sprinkle on the ale yeast. Cover with a piece of muslin and put in a warm place to ferment for 48 hours. Remove the scum. Replace the cloth with an airlock and let the fermentation continue for a further five to six days. Bottle and keep in a cool place.

Use plastic bottles with screw caps. If the fermentation continues without consent, you will notice the bulge. Release the pressure by gently unscrewing the cap. Serve chilled.

WILD THYME *Thymus serpyllum*

Local Names: HORSE TYME, MOTHER OF THYME, TAE-GIRSE,
MOTHER THYME

Season: Throughout the year, but best in summer

Wild Thyme grows on chalk hills, heath and other dry
locations, including sand dunes. Where sheep roam and graze
on Thyme and other herbs their mutton becomes affected, pre-
flavoured so to speak.

Growing up to 10cm tall, Wild Thyme is a low-growing
perennial (*serpyllum* derives from a Greek word 'to creep')
with small opposite oval leaves; flowers are small dense
purple clusters. The aroma is distinctive and just like its cultivated counterpart's, though fainter, as is the flavour. Pick
Wild Thyme in summer when the plant is in flower and its oil,
thymol, at its most volatile.

Traditionally, in the Highlands of Scotland a tea of Thyme
(just put sprigs into boiling water and leave for a minute of
two) was said to banish bad dreams and bring on bravery.
Thyme crushed and put in a bag under the pillow was said to
have the same effect. Thymus is derived from the Greek word
thymon meaning courage; Roman soldiers bathed in Thyme
water before battle. The plant is indigenous to the
Mediterranean. In all likelihood, the Romans brought the herb
with them in their baggage.

The antiseptic and preservative properties of Thyme were
recognised by the Ancient Egyptians, who used it in
embalming. Ancient Greeks employed it as a fumigant; an
alternative derivation for Thyme is from the Greek *thymon*
meaning 'to fumigate'. During the Middle Ages people
clutched sprigs of Thyme to ward off the Plague. By the
sixteenth century the plant had become naturalised in the UK.
A bed of Thyme was thought to be a home to fairies, and
gardeners once set aside a patch of the herb for them, much as
we provide birdhouses. As recently as World War I, the essential oil from Thyme served as a battlefield antiseptic.

The culinary properties of Wild Thyme are almost limitless,
though you will need to use it by the handful to capture the

characteristic savoury pungency. Mix with bay, marjoram and parsley in a *bouquet garni*, and it especially suits slow-cooked dishes of white meat, such as poultry and Shellfish.

To preserve, dry the sprigs, or immerse them in vinegar and olive oil. As with that other 'hard' wild herb Rosemary, Wild Thyme freezes spectacularly well. Simply snip off some branches, wash, pat dry, put in a freezer bag, then into the freezer. The needles conveniently fall off the stems, but smell and taste almost as fresh as the day they were picked.

11

ROAD-KILL

In theory, you could eat just about any animal killed in a traffic accident, from a blackbird to the pussy cat who was chasing it without due attention to the oncoming van. In practice, you are likely to choose to eat only those animals that actually feature in a butcher's display, although Badger is reputed to be more of an epicurean treat than one might assume. Brock's 'hams' are said to be especially tasty.

In practice too, the range of edible animals to be found lying dead by the side of the road is narrowed by their general abundance (or not) in nature, their habits and habitat. Regrettably, I have yet to find a road-kill Red Grouse.

Then there is the small matter of the law. All wild animals have to be killed lawfully, which for birds and beasts in Britain means by a gun in almost all cases. Consequently, if you pick up a wild animal that you have run over yourself you may be prosecuted for killing an animal in an illegal manner. By law, but perhaps not by common sense, someone else has to have run over your road-kill and not you.

Now throw in the Wildlife and Countryside Act: the Act makes it illegal to take or possess pretty much anything and everything wild, whether dead or alive, and no matter how you came by it. The exceptions are game and 'quarry' species. So if you find a dead Pheasant, Partridge, Wood Pigeon, Rabbit, Hare, etc you can keep it.

The three creatures that provide lawful and edible road-kill are the Rabbit, Pheasant and Squirrel; if you do find a Red-Grouse or a Hare, you can easily adapt the instructions below.

The Number 1 rule of preparing road-kill is that you need to see the licence plate of the perpetrating vehicle: the fresher and warmer the corpse, the less likelihood of it having become a haven for parasites and the flesh having begun to rot. Reject any animal positively battered, with ruptured internal organs or with signs of disease. Sick animals are statistically more likely to die a death on the roads, being slower and less alert. That said, there are plenty of Rabbits, Squirrels and Pheasants healthy, young and dumb enough not to know the Green Cross Code.

RABBIT

The Rabbit, like so much else in British life, came over with the Romans; it has been nibbling its way through Mr McGregor's garden produce ever since.

Coney, bunny, call it what you will, the Rabbit has always been food for free, something the peasant could cook in his hovel while the lord of the manor sat down to spit-roast venison. During the world wars of the twentieth century, when rationing was the order of the day, the Rabbit helped keep the nation's stomach from rumbling.

Myxomatosis has devastated the Rabbit population of Britain, which also downs (and ups) according to the weather and the prevalence of predators. Even so, the Rabbit is the edible road-kill most likely to appear on tarmacadam near you, helped by the Rabbit's infamous suicidal tendency to freeze before oncoming headlights.

If you are not squeamish, you can tell the age of Rabbit by the tearability of its ears; the ears of young (thus succulent and tender) Rabbits split easily when pulled.

Rabbit should be hung in a dark, cool place for at least 48 hours before you attend to the gory business of skinning and paunching.

To skin and paunch:
newspaper sheets laid down on a kitchen table
a small sharp knife
a heavy carving knife or secateurs
carrier bag

Lay the Rabbit on its back. Take a sharp knife and cut the skin around all four paws at the first joint. Then slit open the front from anus to breastbone, taking care not to rupture the intestines. Remove the guts and internal organs, starting from the throat and working down. Do this with your fingers, remembering to push into the narrow chest cage to tug out the lights, heart and liver. Make a circular incision around the tail and prise out the bitter gall-bladder. Chop off the Rabbit's head with a heavy carving knife. Now, grip the pelt at the Rabbit's rear end, and pull towards the neck head as though you were pulling its clothes off. The skin will come off in one piece.

With a sharp knife, cut off the yellowish membrane that covers the 'saddle' and hind-quarters; this prevents the meat from cooking, as well as imparting an unpleasant taste.

Some of the 'bits' you have removed from the inside of the Rabbit are edible, such as the heart, but until you have studied form and learned to absolutely distinguish the liver from the kidneys discard into your waiting carrier bag. The organs of wild animals tend to be extremely strong in flavour, and when you are comfortable with your knowledge of an animal's anatomy, you are likely to find they cook better as pâté and stew rather than delicacies by themselves.

Elderly bunny will need a long, slow cook in plenty of liquid, and you can perform some additional tenderizing and whitening by submerging the butchered Rabbit in slightly salted water for a couple of hours; young Rabbit can be treated like chicken, jointed and dusted with flour, before frying or roasting.

Wild Rabbit is fantastically lean mean, and provides good doses of the minerals selenium, iron and zinc.

MUSTARD RABBIT

Serves 4

This is a labour-light recipe, although it does require some planning as the Rabbit needs to soak in water, then in a viscous marinade, which takes upwards of eight hours in total.

1 Rabbit, skinned and cleaned
1 tsp chopped fresh tarragon
250g grainy Dijon mustard
2 tbsp extra virgin olive oil
100g bacon, chopped
1 onion, finely chopped
1 clove garlic, crushed
1 tsp plain flour
570ml vegetable stock

Skin, gut and joint the Rabbit into six pieces, then soak in cold salted water for 2 hours.

Drain and pat dry the Rabbit pieces.

Mix the tarragon with 3 tablespoons of mustard, then smear over the Rabbit bits and leave for at least six hours.

Preheat the oven to 170°C/Gas Mark 3.

Heat the olive oil in a frying pan and brown the Rabbit pieces. Remove the Rabbit pieces and place to one side. Add into the pan the bacon, onion and garlic and cook over a low heat until the onion softens. Stir in the flour with a wooden spoon.

Remove from the heat, and stir in the stock. Then place back on the heat and bring to the boil, stirring continuously.

Place the Rabbit pieces into a casserole, and pour over the sauce from the pan. Cook in the oven until the Rabbit is tender, which will take between 70–90 minutes.

Remove the Rabbit pieces to a warmed serving dish, and check the sauce to see if it requires seasoning. Boil the sauce rapidly to reduce it. Pour over the Rabbit pieces. Garnish with parsley.

SQUIRREL   *Sciurus carolinensis*

Introduced into Britain from North America in the nineteenth century, the Grey Squirrel has run riot, hooliganistically driving out the native Red Squirrel and eating the eggs of woodland birds. Since it frequents city parks as well as the countryside, the Grey Squirrel has the dubious distinction of being the most widespread (as it were) road-kill. An estimated five million Grey Squirrels live in Britain.

Game butchers now sell Grey Squirrels by the lorry load. Although frequently likened on the plate to chicken, they actually taste more like Rabbit; most of the meat, which is lean and firmer than Rabbit, comes from the back legs. Unlike some other 'game', Squirrels should not be hung, and neither should the brains or nervous system be used in your cooking. Squirrels carry the same prions that cause BSE in cattle, and cooking does not properly destroy them. Grey Squirrel can be quite tough, because Squirrels live relatively long – upwards of six years. If the animal is heavy, around a kilo, and you need to play tug-of-war to get the skin off, you have probably collected a mature animal that will require mincing or casseroling, rather than roasting. Matelots in the Royal Navy used to casserole Squirrel in Madeira and onions.

To skin and gut Squirrel:
newspaper, laid on table and floor
a sharp kitchen knife
secateurs or an extremely heavy knife

First of all, if you are a novice, dip the Squirrel in cold water to matt the fur, which will save it from sticking to bits of meat and flying around the room as you cut and gut.

Just as there is more than one way of skinning a cat, there is more than one way of preparing Squirrel. Many, including myself, swear by the following 'sock rolling' technique. Put the Squirrel face down on the board. Pull the tail back towards the head, and slice laterally underneath across the base of the tail to make an incision, taking care not to cut off the tail. Twist the tail round to break it. With the point of your knife under the skin, cut slightly across the back; essentially you are creating a skin flap to pull. Now place the Squirrel front up on the floor (with some newspapers underneath), put your heel on the tail, take a firm hold of the back legs and pull up over the animal's head. Most of the Squirrel will be undressed, except for some skin on the back legs, which can be pulled off easily with your fingers.

What is good about this technique is that it works with older animals, whose skin is notoriously difficult to detach. Put the pelt immediately into a carrier, because it will likely be harbouring lice, especially behind the ears, the last place on a dead animal to cool.

Now place the Squirrel on newspaper on a hard surface, face up. With your sharp knife make a delicate cut along the abdomen, starting at the base of the rib cage. This will expose the innards, which can be pulled out with your fingers. Cut through the diaphragm and remove the lungs, heart, etc. Pull the back legs backwards, breaking the pelvic area and remove the anal intestine. Cut off the head and limbs above the feet. When you have a clean, hollow space you are done, and the animal can be cooked as is, or jointed.

HERBY SQUIRREL BURGERS

Serves 4

1 egg, beaten
450g lean minced Squirrel
1 clove garlic, finely chopped
1 tsp Wild Thyme
1 tsp chervil

1 tsp Worcester sauce
salt and pepper
1 tbsp extra virgin olive oil
4 burger buns
tomato paste

Mix together the egg, meat, herbs, Worcester sauce and salt in a bowl. Shape in flat patties, and fry in the olive oil until cooked, about 5 minutes each side. Serve between buns spread with tomato paste, and green salad.

PHEASANT *Phasianus colchicus*

The Pheasant is a bird of the East, although it has been naturalised in Britain and Europe for centuries. Whether it was the Romans or the Normans who imported the bird is the subject of some dispute in birding circles; certainly the Norman overlords of Britain passed stringent laws to protect Pheasants from the peasants and reserve them as a dish for the aristocratic table. Henry VIII kept a French priest as a 'feausant breeder', but the Tudors used the bird for sport (falconry) as well as filling the royal stomach. Two centuries later, Pheasant numbers declined severely due to woodland clearance but were revived when the bird was reared artificially for shooting with specially developed firearms (shotguns) on country estates. Game shooting has preserved the Pheasant in considerable numbers. The exotic bird of paradise dead on the road is unlikely to be wild, even feral, and was probably a wanderer raised for a shoot. Half wild, then.

How Pheasant is prepared and cooked depends somewhat on its age. Young birds have smooth legs; old birds need to be stewed, and are thus not worth plucking. Pull off the skin and feathers instead. All birds benefit from hanging by the neck for a week in a cool dark place.

How to Skin and Draw a Pheasant for the Oven:
newspaper
sharp kitchen knife
pair of pliers
secateurs

The easiest way to prepare a Pheasant for the oven is to skin it. Put the bird on its back on newspaper on a hard surface, spread out a wing, feel where the wing joins the bird and crack down through the 'shoulder' with a heavy knife. Cut off the other wing in the same fashion, as close to the body as possible. If you lack a heavy knife or biceps, snip off the wings with secateurs.

Now pull out the tail feathers one by one.

Next the legs. Cut around the hinge joint (the 'knee') with a sharp knife, taking care not to cut into the white stringy tendons inside. Now break the leg by snapping it backwards. Hold the bottom of the snapped leg with a pair of pliers and hold the thigh firmly with your other hand. A heavy pull of the pliers will pull the leg off – and with it the white tendons which reach up into the thigh.

It does not matter if you fail to pull the tendons out; they are merely a bit tough to chew.

Repeat the procedure with the other leg.

To detach the head, have the bird on its back and feel where the neck joins the body. You should encounter a hollow with your finger. Wielding the heavy knife, decapitate the bird at this place. With the bird's head and neck removed, wriggle a finger around the neck hole to loosen the innards. You'll encounter the bird's crop in the neck entrance. Pull it out, open it up – and see what the bird had for lunch.

Now to take the skin off. With the bird on its back, pull up a fold of skin and cut an incision you can get your fingers inside. And simply start pulling the skin off, as though you were taking off somebody's overcoat from the front. With the skin off, cut across the anus where the tail feathers were (and where some feathers still likely lurk).

To degut. Put the bird on its back, feel under the rib cage and make a lateral cut across the bird. Don't press down because you do not want to rupture the innards. Then, with your fingers, poke in under the breast bone and pull all the innards out. The first time you gut a bird you are unlikely to get everything out in one motion, so double check that the lungs and kidneys have come too. Effectively, the bird should be empty, and you can see light through the neck. If you are familiar with a bird's anatomy, keep the liver and heart for pâté. Otherwise discard.

Wash the bird under running water and pat dry with a tea towel.

How to Pluck a Pheasant for the Oven:
newspaper
sharp kitchen knife
pair of pliers
draught free room (or sit outside)
dustbin
chair

A warm bird is easier to pluck than one beset with rigor mortis, but if you want as flavoursome and tender a bird as possible it has to be hung to allow the lactic acid to work. So, a cold bird then. Birds, incidentally, keep better with their insides intact. A gutted bird must be cooked within a day or two.

Put the bird on its back on a hard surface, extend a wing, feel for the shoulder joint where wing joins body and cut down through it with a heavy knife. Or snip off with secateurs.

Sit on a chair in a draught-free room, with newspaper on the floor and a dustbin or bucket beside you. Even better, sit outside.

Hold the bird on your lap and tug the feathers of the body with short, sharp motions downwards towards the tail. Work from the tail end up towards the head. Put the feathers into a dustbin if going to the rubbish dump, in a bucket if going to a compost heap. Only de-feather up to the neck, since you will chop this off.

Now follow the instructions for 'drawing' or gutting the Pheasant as on page 193.

POT ROAST PHEASANT IN CIDER

Serves 4

A French-based recipe that works wonders on even the toughest old bird.

2 Pheasants
salt and ground black pepper
2 tbsp extra virgin olive oil
8 dry-cured streaky bacon rashers, rinds removed
4 cloves garlic, peeled and crushed
1 onion, chopped
6 Juniper berries, crushed
1 Cox's apple, peeled, cored and diced
4 Thyme sprigs
2 bay leaves
1 litre traditional dry cider
50g unsalted butter

Preheat the oven to 170°C/Gas Mark 3. Season the pheasants. Heat the oil in a large, ovenproof casserole dish, put in the Pheasants and brown. Remove the Pheasants and place to one side. Put the bacon, plus the garlic, onion, fruit and herbs into the casserole and brown the bacon. Season. Add the cider, bring to the boil, put on the lid and place in the oven. Allow to cook for 30–40 minutes. Once cooked, remove the Pheasants and bacon and allow to rest. Put the casserole dish back on the heat on the stove, remove the lid and let the remaining juices reduce by half by rapid boiling. Cut the butter into small pieces and whisk in.

Carve the Pheasant, allowing one leg and one breast per person, plus two slices of bacon. Spoon over the juices and serve with Savoy cabbage and mash potatoes seasoned with sea salt and black pepper.

12

A WILD FOOD CALENDAR

What To Look Out For When

January–March

Birch (sap)
Bistort (March)
Biting Stonecrop
Bog Myrtle
Brooklime
Chickweed
Chicory (leaves)
Cleavers
Colt's Foot
Dandelion (leaves)
Dead-Nettles (March)
Docks
Dulse
Fat Hen (March)
Fennel (leaves, March)
Garlic Mustard (March)
Ground Elder
Ground Ivy
Hairy Bittercress
Hawthorn (leaves, March)
Herb Bennet
Horseradish
Jew's Ear
Kelp

Lamb's Lettuce
Laver
Lettuce Laver
Lime (sap)
Morel (March)
Nettle
Primrose (March)
Reedmace (roots January,
    shoots February–March)
Salad Burnet
Scurvy Grass
Sea Purslane
Shepherd's Purse
Sorrel
Spruce
Stinging Nettle
Sweet Violet
Tansy
Watercress
Wild Garlic
Wild Parsnips
Wintercress
Wood Sorrel

April–June

Alexanders
Balm
Bistort
Biting Stonecrop
Black Mustard
Bog Myrtle
Borage
Brooklime
Broom
Burdock
Carragheen
Chamomile
Chanterelle
Cleavers
Coltsfoot
Comfrey
Coriander
Corn Salad
Cow Parsley
Cowslip
Dandelion
Dead-Nettle
Dulse
Elder (flowers)
Fairy Ring Mushrooms
Fat Hen
Fennel (leaves)
Field Poppy
Garlic Mustard
Giant Puffball
Good King Henry
Gorse
Ground Elder
Ground Ivy
Hairy Bittercress
Hawthorn (leaves)
Herb Bennet

Hogweed
Hops (shoots)
Horseradish
Ivy-Leaved Toadflax
Jew's Ear
Kelp
Lady's Smock
Laver
Lime
Lovage (leaves)
Mallow
Marsh Samphire
Meadowsweet
Morel
Mugwort
Nettles
Nipplewort
Orache
Pignut (June)
Plantain
Primrose
Reedmace (flowers)
Rock Samphire
Rosebay Willowherb
Rosemary
St. George's Mushroom
Salad Burnet
Scurvy Grass
Sea Beet
Sea Kale
Sea Lettuce
Sea Purslane
Shepherd's Purse
Silverweed
Sorrel
Sow Thistle
Spignel (leaves)
Spruce

Sweet Cecily
Sweet Violet
Tansy
Wall Pennywort
Watercress
Wild Cabbage
Wild Celery (Smallage)
Wild Garlic
Wild Strawberry (June)
Wood Avens and Wood Sorrel
Woodruff
Yarrow

July–September

Agrimony
Ash
Balm
Barbery
Beefsteak Mushroom
Bilberry
Black Mustard
Blackberry
Blackcurrant
Blackthorn (sloes, September)
Bog Myrtle
Borage
Brooklime
Bullace (September)
Burdock
Caraway
Carragheen
Cep
Chamomile
Chickweed
Cloudberry
Comfrey (July)
Coriander
Corn Salad

Crab Apple
Cranberry
Crowberry
Dandelion
Dulse
Elder (berries)
Fairy Ring Mushroom
Fat Hen
Fennel
Field Mushroom
Ground Elder
Ground Ivy
Hairy Bittercress
Hawthorn (berries)
Hazel Nuts (September)
Heather
Hen of the Woods
Herb Bennet
Hogweed
Hops (cones)
Horn of Plenty
Horseradish
Hottentot Fig
Jew's Ear
Juniper (September)
Kelp
Laver
Mallow (leaves)
Marjoram
Marsh Samphire
Meadowsweet
Mugwort
Nipplewort
Parasol Mushroom
Pignut (until July)
Poppy
Red Clover
Rowan

Salad Burnet
Sea Beet
Sea Buckthorn
Sea Lettuce
Sea Purslane
Service Tree
Shaggy Cap Mushrooms
Shepherd's Purse
Silverweed
Sloe
Sorrel
Sow Thistle
Spignel (roots and seeds)
Strawberry
Sweet Cecily
Tansy
Wall Pennywort
Watercress
Wild Celery
Wild Cherry
Wild Garlic (bulbs)
Wild Marjoram
Wild Raspberry
Wild Rose (hips)
Wild Strawberry
Wild Thyme
Wintercress
Wood Blewit
Wood Sorrel
Woodruff
Yarrow

October–December

Alexanders (roots)
Barberry
Beech
Beefsteak Mushroom
Biting Stonecrop
Blackberry
Blackthorn (sloes)
Brooklime
Bullace
Cep
Chanterelle
Chickweed
Corn Salad
Cowberry
Crab Apple
Cranberry
Crowberry
Dandelion (roots)
Dulse
Elder
Fairy Ring Mushroom
Fat Hen
Field Mushroom
Fennel (seeds, roots)
Garlic Mustard (roots)
Hairy Cress
Hawthorn
Hazel
Heather
Herb Bennet
Horn of Plenty
Horseradish (roots)
Jew's Ear
Juniper
Kelp
Laver
Lettuce Laver

Lovage (seeds)
Medlar
Oak (acorns)
Oyster Mushroom
Parasol Mushroom
Poppy
Redcurrant
Reedmace (roots)
Rosemary
Rowan
Salad Burnet
Sea Lettuce
Sea Purslane
Service Tree
Shaggy Caps Mushroom
Shepherd's Purse
Silverweed
Sorrel
Spignel (roots)
Sweet Cecily
Sweet Chestnut
Walnut
Watercress
Wild Carrot
Wild Rose
Wintercress
Wood Blewit
Yarrow

13

WILD FOOD BY TYPE

Flowers

Alexanders
Borage
Broom
Bullace
Chamomile
Chicory
Coltsfoot
Cowslip
Dandelion
Elder
Heather
Hop
Lime
Mallow
Meadowsweet
Primrose
Red Clover
Red Dead-Nettle
Reedmace
Sweet Violet
Wild Rose

Fruit

Barberry
Bilberry (Whortleberry)
Blackberry
Blackcurrant
Blackthorn
Bullace
Cherry
Cloudberry
Cowberry
Crab Apple
Cranberry
Crowberry
Dewberry
Dog Rose
Elder
Gooseberry
Guelder Rose
Hawthorn
Hottentot Fig
Juniper
Medlar
Oregon Grape
Raspberry
Redcurrant
Rowan (Mountain Ash)
Sea Buckthorn
Service Tree
Whitebeam
Wild Cherry
Wild Rose
Wild Strawberry

Fungi

Amethyst Deceiver
Aniseed Agaric
Beefsteak Fungus
Black Morel
Cauliflower Fungus
Cep
Chanterelle
Chicken of the Woods
Common Stinkhorn
Dryad's Saddle
Fairy Ring Mushroom
Field Blewit
Field Mushroom
Giant Puffball
Hen of the Woods
Horn of Plenty
Horse Mushroom
Jew's Ear
Morel
Oyster
Parasol Mushroom
Pig's Ears
Plums and Custard
St George's Mushroom
Shaggy Ink Cap
Summer Truffle
Tawny Gisette
Winter Chanterelle
Wood Blewitt

Greens and Vegetables

Agrimony
Alexanders
Asparagus
Bath Asparagus
Bistort
Biting Stonecrop
Black Mustard
Bladder Campion
Borage
Brooklime
Burdock
Chickweed
Chicory
Cleavers
Comfrey
Common Valerian
Corn Salad
Cow Parsley
Curled Dock
Dandelion
Dead-Nettle (White and Red)
Dock
Fat Hen
Fennel
Field Pennycress
Garlic Mustard
Golden Saxifrage
Good King Henry
Ground Elder
Hairy Bittercress
Hogweed
Horseradish
Horsetails
Ivy-Leaved Toadflax
Lady's Smock
Lovage
Mallow

Marsh Samphire
Milk Thistle
Nettle
Nipplewort
Orache
Oyster Plant
Parsley Piert
Pigweed
Reedmace
Ribwort Plantain
Rock Samphire
Rosebay Willowherb
Rough Hawkbit
Salad Burnet
Scurvy Grass
Sea Beet
Sea Kale
Sea Purslane
Shepherd's Purse
Sorrel
Sow Thistle
Sweet Cicely
Wall Pennywort
Watercress
White Dead-Nettle
White Mustard
Wild Cabbage
Wild Celery
Wild Garlic
Wintercress
Wood Sorrel
Yarrow

Herbs

Alexanders
Balm
Bog Myrtle
Borage
Chamomile
Chives
Coriander
Cow Parsley
Fennel
Ground Elder
Ground Ivy
Herb Bennet
Juniper
Marjoram
Mugwort
Orache
Rosemary
Salad Burnet
Sand Leek
Shepherd's Purse
Spignel
Spruce
Tansy
Water Mint
Wild Garlic
Wild Thyme
Wormwood
Woodruff
Yarrow

Nuts and Seeds

Ash (seeds)
Beech
Caraway
Fennel
Garlic Mustard
Hazel
Lovage
Oak (acorns)
Poppy
Spignel
Sweet Chestnut
Walnut

Roots

Arrow Head
Bitter Vetch
Chicory
Dandelion
Dittander
Early Purple Orchid
Evening Primrose
Fennel
Garlic Mustard
Goat's-Beard
Horseradish
Pignut
Reedmace
Restharrow
Salsify
Sea Holly
Silverweed
Spignel
White Water Lily
Wild Carrot
Wild Garlic
Wild Parsnip

Seaweed

Batter Frond
Bladder Wrack
Carragheen
Dulse
Gutweed
Kelp (Oarweed)
Laver
Pepper Dulse
Sea Lettuce
Sugar Kelp

FURTHER INFORMATION

Courses
For an online guide to foraging courses see
www.foodforagingcourses.co.uk
Expert foragers Nick Weston and Andy R Hamilton both
run courses and can be contacted respectively at
www.huntergathercook.com and
www.theotherandyhamilton.com

Bibliography
Ian Burrows, *Food from the Wild*, 2011
T. Cameron, *The Wild Foods of Great Britain*, 1917
Andrew C. Campbell, *Philip's Guide to Seashores and
    Shallow Seas of Britain and Europe*, 2005
Antonio Carlucci, *Goes Wild*, 2001
Ceres, *Free for All*, 1977
Paul Chambers, *Foraging*, 2010
Allen Coombes, *Pocket Nature Trees*, 2010
R. Courtecuisse, *Collins Guide to the Mushrooms of Britain
    and Europe*, 1999
Nicholas Culpeper, *The English Physician*, 1770
John Gerard, *Great Herball*, 1633
Geoffrey Grigson *The Englishman's Flora*, 1975
Andy R Hamilton, *Booze for Free*, 2011
Jason Hill, *Wild Foods of Great Britain*, 1939
Fiona Houston and Xa Milne, *Seaweed and Eat It: A Family*

Foraging and Cooking Adventure, 2008
Richard Mabey, *Food for Free*, 2001
Vicomte De Mauduit, *They Can't Ration These*, 2004
Roger Phillips, *Wild Food*, 1983
Francis Rose and Clare O'Reilly, *The Wild Flower Key:
How to Identify Wild Plants, Trees and Shrubs in Britain
and Ireland*, 2006
David Squire, *Self Sufficiency Foraging*, 2011
John Griffith Vaughan, Catherine Geissler, *The New Oxford
Book of Food Plants*, 2009
Nick Weston *The Tree House Diaries*, 2010
John Wright, *The River Cottage Edible Seashore Handbook*,
2009

Websites
www.bushcraft-magazine.co.uk

Organisations
Natural England
www.naturalengland.org.uk 0114 241 8920
Countryside Council for Wales
www.ccw.gov.uk 0845 106229
Scottish Natural Heritage
www.snh.org.uk 01463 725000
**Department for Environment, Food and Rural Affairs
(DEFRA)**
www.defra.gov.uk 0845 933 5577
National Trust
www.nationaltrust.org.uk 0844 800 1895
National Trust for Scotland
www.nts.org.uk 0844 493 2100
Crown Estate
www.thecrownestate.co.uk 0207 851 5000
Marine Stewardship Council
www.msc.org

INDEX